Life

During the Renaissance

Titles in The Way People Live series include:

THE WAY
PEOPLE
LIVE

Life During the Renaissance

by Patricia D. Netzley

Lucent Books, P.O. Box 289011, San Diego, CA 92198-9011

With appreciation for the Faber family,
and for Raymond, Matthew, Sarah, and Jacob Netzley,
whose love and support I treasure

Library of Congress Cataloging-in-Publication Data

Netzley, Patricia D.
    Life during the Renaissance / by Patricia D. Netzley.
        p.   cm. — (The way people live)
    Includes bibliographical references and index.
    Summary: Describes the history, culture, and life of people living during
the Renaissance.
    ISBN 1-56006-375-0 (alk. paper)
    1. Renaissance—Juvenile literature.   [1. Renaissance.]   I. Title.
II. Series.
    CB353.N39   1998
    940.2'1—dc21   97-39781
                                                                                     CIP
                                                                                      AC

Contents

Discovering the Humanity in Us All

The Way People Live series focuses on pockets of human culture. Some of these are current cultures, like the Eskimos of the Arctic; others no longer exist, such as the Jewish ghetto in Warsaw during World War II. What many of these cultural pockets share, however, is the fact that they have been viewed before, but not completely understood.

To really understand any culture, it is necessary to strip the mind of the common notions we hold about groups of people. These stereotypes are the archenemies of learning. It does not even matter whether the stereotypes are positive or negative; they are confining and tight. Removing them is a challenge that's not easily met, as anyone who has ever tried it will admit. Ideas that do not fit into the templates we create are unwelcome visitors—ones we would prefer remain quietly in a corner or forgotten room.

The cowboy of the Old West is a good example of such confining roles. The cowboy was courageous, yet soft-spoken. His time (it is always a he, in our template) was spent alternatively saving a rancher's daughter from certain death on a runaway stagecoach, or shooting it out with rustlers. At times, of course, he was likely to get a little crazy in town after a trail drive, but for the most part, he was the epitome of inner strength. It is disconcerting to find out that the cowboy is human, even a bit childish. Can it really be true that cowboys would line up to help the cook on the trail drive grind coffee, just hoping he would give them a little stick of pep-

permint candy that came with the coffee shipment? The idea of tough cowboys vying with one another to help "Coosie" (as they called their cooks) for a bit of candy seems silly and out of place.

So is the vision of Eskimos playing video games and watching MTV, living in prefab housing in the Arctic. It just does not fit with what "Eskimo" means. We are far more comfortable with snow igloos and whale blubber, harpoons and kayaks.

Although the cultures dealt with in Lucent's The Way People Live series are often historically and socially well known, the emphasis is on the personal aspects of life. Groups of people, while unquestionably affected by their politics and their governmental structures, are more than those institutions. How do people in a particular time and place educate their children? What do they eat? And how do they build their houses? What kinds of work do they do? What kinds of games do they enjoy? The answers to these questions bring these cultures to life. People's lives are revealed in the particulars and only by knowing the particulars can we understand these cultures' will to survive and their moments of weakness and greatness.

This is not to say that understanding politics does not help to understand a culture. There is no question that the Warsaw ghetto, for example, was a culture that was brought about by the politics and social ideas of Adolf Hitler and the Third Reich. But the Jews who were crowded together in the ghetto cannot be understood by the Reich's politics. Their life was a day-to-day battle for existence, and the creativity and methods they used to prolong their lives is a vital story of human perseverance that would be denied by focusing only on the institutions of Hitler's Germany. Knowing that children as young as five or six outwitted Nazi guards on a daily basis, that Jewish policemen helped the Germans control the ghetto, that children attended secret schools in the ghetto and even earned diplomas—these are the things that reveal the fabric of life, that can inspire, intrigue, and amaze.

Books in The Way People Live series allow both the casual reader and the student to see humans as victims, heroes, and onlookers. And although humans act in ways that can fill us with feelings of sorrow and revulsion, it is important to remember that "hero," "predator," and "victim" are dangerous terms. Heaping undue pity or praise on people reduces them to objects, and strips them of their humanity.

Seeing the Jews of Warsaw only as victims is to deny their humanity. Seeing them only as they appear in surviving photos, staring at the camera with infinite sadness, is limiting, both to them and to those who want to understand them. To an object of pity, the only appropriate response becomes "Those poor creatures!" and that reduces both the quality of their struggle and the depth of their despair. No one is served by such two-dimensional views of people and their cultures.

With this in mind, The Way People Live series strives to flesh out the traditional, two-dimensional views of people in various cultures and historical circumstances. Using a wide variety of primary quotations—the words not only of the politicians and government leaders, but of the real people whose lives are being examined—each book in the series attempts to show an honest and complete picture of a culture removed from our own by time or space.

By examining cultures in this way, the reader will notice not only the glaring differences from his or her own culture, but also will be struck by the similarities. For indeed, people share common needs—warmth, good company, stability, and affirmation from others. Ultimately, seeing how people really live, or have lived can only enrich our understanding of ourselves.

A Break with the Past: New Ideas and Beliefs

The Renaissance—a term that means rebirth—is the period in European history marked by a renewed interest in classical scholarship and art forms that had been forsaken by much of society during the Middle Ages. Along with the rediscovery of ancient knowledge came changes in class structure, government, and trade.

The Renaissance began in Italy in approximately 1300 and gradually spread to central and northern Europe and England during the next 350 years. However, historians typically define the period not in terms of strict dates but in terms of changes in social relations, econom ics, and thought. Historian Kenneth Atchity explains that many consider the Renaissance to represent "a sharp break with the Middle Ages,"[1] because medieval beliefs and practices underwent a dramatic shift in the Renaissance.

The Pursuit of Knowledge

For example, during the Middle Ages, education had little value among common people because it did not help a person better his position in life. Those in power were born to rule; feudal rulers and nobles controlled most of the

Categorizing People

Renaissance people and cultures varied widely, and it was common to categorize individuals based on their appearance and place of birth. John Hale, in his book The Civilization of Europe in the Renaissance, *quotes a comparison of Spaniards and Frenchmen written by a biased Spanish writer, Carlos Garcia, in 1617.*

"The Spanish are bodily so different, and so contrasted with the French that it would be a waste of time to dwell on it, for most Spaniards are small, most Frenchmen tall; the French are blonde, the Spaniards dark; the complexion of the French is pale or rosy, the Spaniards swarthy; the French wear their hair long, the Spaniards short; the French have slim legs, the Spaniard's legs so sturdy that a Spaniard's calf is as thick as a Frenchman's thigh; the French let their beards grow unshaven from one temple round to the other, the Spaniards shave it, leaving only a moustache and a brush under the lip; the French are choleric, the Spaniards patient; the French are sprightly, the Spaniards slow to act; the former are volatile, cheerful and impetuous, the latter are ponderous, sombre and introspective; the French eat a lot, the Spanish little, the French are givers, the Spaniards savers— one could go on comparing the one with the other and find nothing but contraries."

An increase in trade during the Renaissance created a large merchant class. Merchants stimulated Renaissance society because they had money to spend on business, education, and the arts.

land and its wealth. Peasants struggling to survive as tenant farmers or in the ranks of armies had no class mobility and no time to indulge in the pursuit of knowledge. Meanwhile, the Catholic Church greatly influenced behavior, promoting self-sacrifice, humility, and devotion to duty. These attitudes, along with the harsh living conditions of farm life, discouraged creativity and personal exploration.

In contrast, the Renaissance is noted for inquiry and an expansion of knowledge, as well as its emphasis on the value of the individual. Renaissance creativity produced some of the world's greatest art and literature. Science and medicine also advanced dramatically. The declining influence of the Catholic

Church freed people to follow their own interests and allowed greater self-expression.

Economic Influences

However, the interest in education was also influenced by a changing economy. For different reasons in different countries, agriculture was becoming less lucrative, and many farmers decided to move to the cities to take up new occupations. However, to succeed in a trade they needed to know how to read and perform bookkeeping tasks. Therefore education became more important, and parents of a growing merchant class increasingly wanted

A Break with the Past: New Ideas and Beliefs **9**

their children to attend not just grammar schools but universities. In such institutions students were exposed to ways of thinking that had been lost or ignored by the populace of the Middle Ages.

The Renaissance economy also stimulated the creative arts. The Renaissance merchant economy allowed members of the lower classes to become wealthy, and these newly rich wanted the trappings and the sophistication of the aristocracy. They became patrons of the arts and bought many fine paintings and decorative tapestries for their homes. As the value of such items rose, artists became important members of the community, and middle- and upper-class fathers increasingly encouraged their sons to learn to paint. Wealthy merchants also supported scientific investigation, architectural projects, and voyages of exploration to increase their social status as well as their income.

However, not everyone in the Renaissance reaped the benefits of the new merchant economy. Those who remained on the farm found life much the same as in the Middle Ages. In fact, in some agricultural regions the Renaissance economy devastated farmers. For example, as the wool industry grew in importance, more landowners in England decided to raise sheep instead of growing crops. They therefore needed fewer farmworkers, and many peasants lost their livelihoods.

"A New Era"

Where poverty was widespread, creative pursuits were of little or no importance, and in most places there were still far more poor than rich. Farmers and unskilled city dwellers alike had little chance to benefit from the new merchant economy. For this reason, historian John McKay, unlike Kenneth Atchity, believes that "in terms of the way most people lived and thought, no sharp division exists between the Middle Ages and the Renaissance."[2] However, he adds that most Renaissance people were very aware that they were "living in a new era," a special time when great changes were occurring. They had a sense of history, and believed that their society would eventually shape the future.

Manorial Duties: The Relationship Between Rural Peasants and Nobles

Throughout the Renaissance, approximately 80 percent of the people lived in small rural villages, typically with populations of less than one hundred, and spaced fifteen miles or more apart. According to historian William Manchester, "In the early 1500s one could hike through the woods for days without encountering a settlement of any size."[3] However, only a few people owned land; the majority paid rent to an aristocratic landlord under a system of services and obligations called manorialism.

Manorialism

Manorialism had its roots in the Middle Ages. At that time, feudalism was the prevailing social structure, which meant that monarchs gave their knights land in exchange for their services during battle. As the military elite, these nobles had a great deal of power, and peasants often needed the protection of a noble to survive. They therefore bound themselves as serfs to a member of the aristocracy, farming his land in exchange for his protection.

Superstitious Peasants

Peasants were both religious and superstitious, which often meant they were easily influenced. In his book The Civilization of Europe in the Renaissance, *John Hale quotes one 1470s German writer.*

"There came to the village of Niklashausen a cowherd and drum player . . . the whole country, he said, was mired in sin and wantonness, and unless our people were ready to do penance and change their wicked ways, God would let all Germany go to destruction. This vision, he said, was revealed to him by the Virgin Mary . . . Thus it came to pass that great numbers of people went to Niklashausen to pray in the church of Our Lady there. All Germany seemed in commotion. Stableboys ran from their horses, taking away the bridles. Reapers left their reaping, carrying their scythes. Women ceased haying, coming with their rakes. Wives left husbands, husbands wives. . . . [Eventually] the drummer and one or two others were burned at the stake and their ashes thrown into the river . . . so that no superstitious cult might be made of them. All the same, a few of the faithful succeeded one night in digging up some soil from the spot where the drummer had been burned. They carried this to their homes and treasured it as a sacred relic."

Serfs harvest grapes in the vineyard of a medieval castle. Although the Renaissance ended serfdom, peasants were still tied to the land and had limited economic opportunities.

Historian John McKay offers some examples of the debts inherent to serfdom:

> In France, England, Germany, and Italy, local custom determined precisely what those services were, but certain practices were common everywhere. The peasant was obliged to turn over to the lord a percentage of the annual harvest, usually in produce, sometimes in cash. The peasant paid a fee to marry someone outside the lord's estate. To inherit property the peasant paid a fine, often the best beast the person owned. Above all, the peasant

became part of the lord's permanent labor force.[4]

During the Renaissance, peasants who worked for the nobility fought for and gained more rights than the serfs who toiled during the Middle Ages. Peasant uprisings were common during the Renaissance. For example, in Florence, Italy, poor workers called *ciompi* revolted in 1378, and Spain had several peasant uprisings in 1391. In England, a large revolt involving perhaps one thousand peasants was put down in 1381, but unrest continued; by 1550 all rural serfdom in that country had ended. The end of serfdom was an important difference between the two periods. In the Middle Ages, peasants who farmed a piece of land were considered a part of that land. When a nobleman sold a farm, his peasants were part of the transaction. But during the Renaissance, most countries abandoned serfdom, and peasants were free to decide where they would live and work. Many decided to remain on their lord's manor and continue the lifestyle they had known. Thus feudalism became manorialism.

The Power of Money

Where rebellion did not end serfdom, money did. Nobles discovered that they could make more income from freemen. Historian Irma Simonton Black explains:

> The nobles constantly needed money . . . [and] they often found that they made more money by collecting a yearly rent in money from free men working their land than by having to bother with all the [bartered goods and services] . . . that the serfs had paid for so long. And they found that free men worked harder on the land

than did a man bound to servitude, no matter how capable he might be.[5]

Challenging the Power of the Nobility

But even after serfdom was abolished, nobles held a great deal of power over peasants, and this relationship would remain unchanged throughout the Renaissance. In fact, according to historian McKay, "Despite political, scientific, and industrial revolutions, the nobility continued to hold real political and social power in Europe down to the nineteenth century." He explains that although the nobles' position in society varied according to location, certain generalizations applied widely:

> Members of the nobility enjoyed a special legal status. A nobleman . . . had immunity from almost all outside authorities. . . . He held courts that dispensed a sort of justice. Sometimes he coined money for use within his territories. . . . He was the political, military, and judicial lord of the people who settled on his lands. He made political decisions affecting them, resolved disputes among them, and protected them in time of attack. . . . [These rights and duties] were inheritable, perpetuated by blood and not by wealth alone.[6]

Because nobles retained such absolute power, peasant revolts did not end after serfdom disappeared. Many peasants chafed against high rents and taxation and wanted some of the nobles' special privileges revoked.

For example, in 1525 many German peasants protested the unfairness of high rents and the nobles' exclusive rights to hunt, fish, and enjoy other benefits on their land. According to historian Henry Lucas:

The peasants drew up numerous documents setting forth their grievances. . . . [They] were to be allowed to hunt and fish, water rights were to be left to the community, in certain cases woods were to revert to the people, . . . a fair price was to be paid for labor, rents were to be just.[7]

When the German nobles refused to meet the peasants' demands, the peasants responded by destroying private lands. As the rebellion grew, German religious reformer and founder of Protestantism Martin Luther tried to intervene. He wrote a pamphlet calling for peace on both sides, but the violence

Despite peasant unrest and competition from the new merchant class, the nobility maintained its hold on economic and political power during the Renaissance.

only escalated. Eventually the German rulers sent the military to end the so-called Peasants' War, and thousands of peasants were killed.

The Fortunes of the New Peasantry

In many places, then, rural peasants were forced to endure economic oppression. However, some did earn enough money from selling their harvest and keeping livestock to better their situation in life. Sometimes a frugal peasant saved enough money to purchase land from a nobleman in financial straits. Once free from having to pay rent, that peasant might then be able to afford the materials to build a small cottage.

From generation to generation, his family would improve itself until one day it could afford to employ others to help with farming, thereby becoming a member of a higher class. Historian John Hale explains that while "profits on farming were small and holdings could be built up only slowly, generation by generation," there were no rules that kept a peasant from moving up in social status; "only local judgment and a reasonable prosperity" determined a person's place in life. [8]

However, a downward move in status was more likely. Changing fortunes often led people into debt. If a borrower did not pay the money back to a lender, he descended in class from free peasant down to indentured servant. Historian Yves Castan says:

> Debt, even when contracted for a limited term only, sometimes created a deliberate servitude, subjecting the unpunctual debtor to taxation, forced labor, and the whim of his creditor. The debtor understood quite well that his best hope of avoiding the worst—seizure of his property by the creditor—was to make the debt agreeable and even profitable. Thus he freely offered his services, allowed his creditor to gather fruit from his orchard, vineyard, or garden, and willingly submitted to various controls on his expenditures. [9]

It was therefore extremely difficult for a peasant to improve his economic situation. However, one condition did make such a person more valuable: a scarcity of workers. Wherever populations were low, the peasants

A peasant tends to his lord's livestock. As increasing numbers of peasants moved to the cities during the Renaissance, there was a demand for people to perform such menial duties.

The Chance to Own Land

Rural peasants led harsh lives and welcomed new opportunities to improve their economic and social positions. Historian Philippe Erlanger discusses the peasants of Renaissance France in his book The Age of Courts and Kings.

"What can be said of the peasants—that multitude of men dragging out their existence in endless toil from which they themselves were not to benefit? What can be said of these victims who were given over to the rigours of tax-collectors, . . . the avarice of usurers, . . . the abuses of noblemen and prelates. . . . If necessary, [the peasant] would harness his wife and children (from the age of ten!) to the plough, he would harness himself to it, 'all dressed in canvas like a windmill'. He suffered and toiled. . . . But if, suddenly, the rainbow shone, if destiny . . . allowed him a moment's respite, he . . . found his good humour intact; and out of his rotten mattress he brought the [money] which would make him a landholder despite his persecutors."

enjoyed more benefits. In such places, peasants could earn good wages for a day's work in the fields, and were thereby able to improve their living conditions more quickly than peasants in overpopulated areas.

The Black Death

Ironically, one of the biggest economic boosts to the lower classes was the bubonic plague, or Black Death. In 1347 the Black Death first appeared in Italy, introduced via sailing vessels from Asian ports, carried in fleas that lived on shipboard rats. In the cities, poor sanitation and overcrowding allowed these fleas to spread rapidly, and through their bites the Black Death spread too.

It was a gruesome disease. McKay reports: "Fourteenth-century medical literature indicates that physicians could sometimes ease the pain, but they had no cure." According to McKay, rough estimates of mortality rates show that it had a devastating effect on population:

Of a total English population of perhaps 4.2 million, probably 1.4 million died of the Black Death in its several visits. Densely populated Italian cities endured incredible losses. Florence lost between half and two-thirds of its 1347 population of 85,000 when the plague visited in 1348. The disease recurred intermittently in the 1360s and 1370s and reappeared many times down to 1700.[10]

McKay asserts that the Black Death ultimately benefited peasants by eliminating overpopulation among the peasant classes and making strong, healthy workers more valuable:

Population decline meant a sharp increase in per capita wealth. Increased demand for labor meant greater mobility among peasant and working classes. Wages rose, providing better distribution of income. The shortage of labor and steady requests for higher wages put landlords on the defensive. . . . They retaliated with . . . measures . . . [that] attempted to

A plague victim indicates characteristic swellings to his physicians. The Black Death decimated populations across Europe, making strong laborers a scarce and valuable commodity.

freeze salaries and wages . . . [but these measures ultimately failed].[11]

In this way, the Black Death was one more reason why rural peasants enjoyed more freedoms during the Renaissance. As demand for workers grew, they could travel from farm to farm to find the best economic position.

The Manor Farm

In fact, however, most peasants never traveled farther than twenty-five miles from the village of their birth. They had strong social ties to their communities, and could not imagine living anywhere else.

In many places, peasant villages were located within a noble's estate, which was called a manor. Manors could be as small as one hundred acres or as large as several thousand acres and typically encompassed a mixture of cultivated and uncultivated land. Forests provided wood, nuts, and berries; pastures and meadows offered grazing for livestock; and lakes and rivers gave water and fish. But the largest acreage was devoted to agriculture, apportioned among the peasants and the noble, although the noble did no farming himself. Instead the peasants collectively worked both his land and theirs.

The relationship between a group of peasants and their nobleman varied according to the customs of a region and the disposition of its nobility. However, in many places the peasants were closely supervised by their employer, whether they worked in the fields or in a nobleman's home as a household servant. For example, according to historian Madeleine Foisil, the journal of one French noble reveals "the familiarity that existed between the rural master and his servants, who lived nearby and whose families mingled constantly both at home and in the fields. Orders were given for each day's task, wages were paid by the master personally, and men and women worked together in fields, meadows, and woods."[12]

Crops were planted on a rotational basis, with half the fields under cultivation and half lying fallow to prolong soil fertility. Some fields were planted with winter crops and the rest with spring crops, so that the land would produce food year-round. Chicken, sheep, and, when available, cow manure were used as fertilizers, and compost from organic household waste was also spread over crops.

Tool lists from the fourteenth century indicate that pitchforks, spades, axes, plows, and harrows, which have teeth to break up soil, were widely used. Both plows and harrows could be pushed or pulled by peasants. However, during the Renaissance an increasing number of farms used horses for such tasks, as well as for pulling carts that would take surplus food to market in nearby towns.

In good years, manor farms provided enough vegetables to make a considerable profit at such markets, particularly in regions where birth rates were rebounding from the Black Death and there was a rising demand for food.

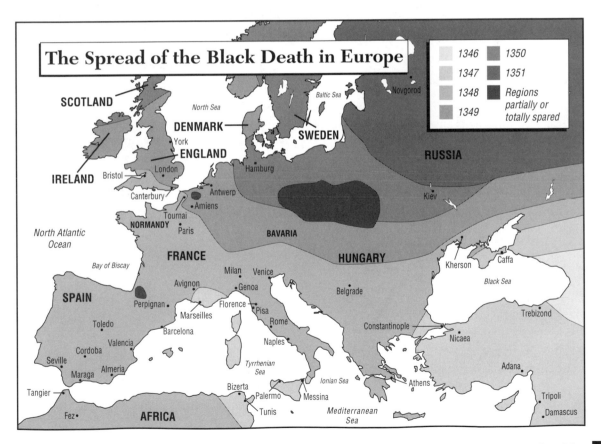

The Spread of the Black Death in Europe

	1346		1350
	1347		1351
	1348		Regions partially or totally spared
	1349		

During the Renaissance, most people ate only two meals a day. Grains, including wheat, oats, rye, and barley, were the primary staples of the Renaissance diet.

Simple Food

Most Renaissance people, peasant and nobleman alike, relied on grains as their main source of nourishment. They subsisted primarily on wheat, oats, barley, and rye, and the most common meal was bread and vegetable soup.

Peasant families ate pork, beef, or game only a few times a year; fowl and eggs were eaten far more often. Milk, butter, and hard cheeses were too expensive for the average peasant. As for vegetables, the most common were cabbage and watercress. Wild carrots were also popular in some places. Parsnips became widespread by the sixteenth century, and German writings from the mid-1500s indicate that beet roots were a preferred food there. Rutabagas were developed during the Middle Ages by crossing turnips with cabbage, and monastic gardens were known for their asparagus and artichokes. However, as a New World vegetable, the potato was not introduced into Europe until the late 1500s or

early 1600s, and for a long time it was thought to be merely a decorative plant.

Most people ate only two meals a day. In most places, water was not the normal beverage. In Italy and France people drank wine, in Germany and England ale or beer. William Manchester notes: "Under [Kings] Henry VII and Henry VIII the per capita allowance was a gallon of beer a day—even for nuns and eight-year-old children. Sir John Fortescue observed that the English 'drink no water, unless at certain times upon religious score, or by way of doing penance.'"[13]

In fact, brewing beer and ale was a main occupation for rural women in England. Historian John McKay reports:

Women dominated in the production of beer and ale for the community market. This industry required an initial investment in large vessels and knowledge of the correct proportions of barley, water, yeast, and hops. Women found brewing a hard and dangerous work: it involved

Elaborate Celebrations

In *A History of Private Life, Jean-Louis Flandrin reports that at large celebrations, hosts typically served dozens of elaborate dishes. For example, at one 1690 banquet, a duke offered* "16 soups, 13 entrees, and 28 hors d'oeuvres in the first course, and 16 meats, 13 side dishes, and 28 hors d'oeuvres in the second course. Add to that no fewer than 57 desserts, for a total of 171 dishes, some quite substantial, for 42 guests." *However, Flandrin explains that this does not mean that people* "ate like pigs."

"Most guests were content simply to sample one dish that happened to be located near where they were seated. . . . Old cookbooks and butler's manuals clearly state that the reason for the large number of dishes was to accommodate the diversity of tastes. [One cookbook] recommends arranging the dishes so that 'each person can take whatever suits his appetite.' It was important to 'avoid placing two similarly prepared dishes close together, without another dish of a different kind in between. To do otherwise would be ungracious and might constrain the taste of some at table, different people liking different things.'"

For the nobility and the most prominent merchants, large banquets were a show of wealth.

carrying 12-gallon vats of hot liquid. Records of the English coroners' courts reveal that 5 percent of women who died lost their lives in brewing accidents, by falling into the vats of boiling liquid.[14]

Noble Privileges

Noblemen enjoyed a more varied diet than the poor, particularly in meats. For example, in most countries, only the nobles were allowed to hunt certain types of game. McKay reports: "In many places there were severe laws against hunting and trapping in the forests. Deer, wild boars, and other game were strictly reserved for the king and nobility. These laws were flagrantly violated, however, and stolen rabbits and wild game often found their way to the peasants' tables."[15]

Nobles also forbade peasants to fish in their lakes or rivers. And because pork was preserved in salt and salting was expensive, few peasants could afford to eat it. Instead they would raise pigs only to sell them to nobles.

In addition to enjoying more foods on a daily basis, nobles also occasionally hosted feasts with many unusual dishes. For example, one Italian banquet offered meat and fowl prepared in 118 different ways, served over several courses, which was typical of Renaissance parties. Historian Philippe Erlanger reports that at German celebrations "the . . . middle class served six courses, each of nine different dishes. The upper class served only three courses, but each consisted of 100 items."[16] Erlanger adds that in many places "there was no fixed order for the procession of dishes."[17] However, he says that the usual sequence in France was soups, salads, and hashes, followed by meats and fowl, and then dessert, fruits, cheeses, and other delicacies.

Housing Discrepancies

Not only food but also housing differed between nobles and peasants. Noblemen and their families typically resided in large stone houses of many rooms, with large fireplaces, fine wall tapestries and rugs, and a great deal of furniture. Almost everyone had his or her own bed.

Throughout Europe, possessing a bed was considered a mark of status, and the beds of the most privileged were quite ornate, with a canopy on top, four velvet curtains draping its sides, and an elaborate headboard that might be inlaid with precious stones. These beds could be as large as eight feet in length and seven feet in width. Bedding was of silk or other fine fabrics. Mattresses had no springs or fixed frame; they were simply cloth bags of goose down, straw, dried peas, or leaves, depending on the status of the owner.

In contrast, most peasants could not afford a bed, or even a mattress. They slept on the floor, on straw or rush mats, covered by thin blankets. Those who could afford a bed had to share it with all family members. Historian William Manchester says that in a typical one-room peasant home,

> The centerpiece of the room was a gigantic bedstead, piled high with straw pallets, all seething with vermin. Everyone slept there, regardless of age or gender—grandparents, parents, children, grandchildren, and hens and pigs. . . . If a stranger was staying the night, hospitality required that he be invited to make "one more" on the familial mattress.[18]

Most peasants lived in cramped conditions in a house made of flimsy materials. William Manchester offers this description of the poorest peasant homes:

A painting by Jan Brueghel the Elder, dated circa 1597, depicts a landlord and his wife (left) paying a visit to their peasant tenants. The large common rooms of peasant houses were often chaotic because family members cherished the warmth of the fire when conducting their household chores.

Some lived in tiny cabins of crossed laths stuffed with grass or straw, inadequately shielded from rain, snow, and wind. They lacked even a chimney; smoke from the cabin's fire left through a small hole in the thatched roof—where, unsurprisingly, fires frequently broke out. These homes were without glass windows or shutters; in a storm, or in frigid weather, openings in the walls could only be stuffed with straw, rags—whatever was handy.[19]

Manchester adds that sanitary conditions in these houses were also poor. He quotes Dutch Renaissance scholar Erasmus as saying that "almost all the floors are of clay and rushes from the marshes, so carelessly renewed that the foundation sometimes remains for twenty years, harboring, there below, spittle and vomit and wine of dogs and men, beer, . . . remnants of fishes, and other filth unnameable. Hence, with the change of weather, a vapor exhales which in my judgment is far from wholesome."[20]

However, some prosperous peasants did own multiroom or even two-story houses, with separate bedrooms for parents and children, and could afford sheds to house their animals. As for household size, although it varied according to region, generally people lived in a nuclear family, which means a married couple and their children. Grandparents and other extended relatives lived elsewhere. For example, McKay reports: "The simple family predominated in . . . northern France in the fourteenth century, and in fifteenth-century Tuscany [Italy]. . . . The typical household numbered about five people, the parents and three children."[21]

Moving to the City

Peasant families were close-knit. However, as the Black Death swept through village after village, it became difficult for young peasants to find spouses. The fragmentation of families by illness, coupled with new economic mobility, led many young men to move to the city.

In England, many noblemen encouraged this migration by converting their land to raising livestock rather than farming, evicting their tenants and closing down entire villages. Historian Sarah Howarth quotes English statesman and author (and Catholic saint) Sir Thomas More's complaint: "Sheep now eat up fields and houses. Their owners enclose all the land, throw down houses and leave nothing standing but the church."[22]

Poland, France, and Germany also had many deserted villages, although, as Howarth explains, "the reasons for this varied from country to country."[23] Sometimes a village was abandoned because the surrounding soils were depleted and ceased to yield good crops. In other locations, the decline in population caused by the Black Death lowered food prices and made farming unprofitable.

But whatever the reason, once a village was abandoned, most of its peasants headed for the city to try to make their living. And as migration increased and the cities grew in size and importance, many noblemen decided to move there too. Historian John McKay believes that the upper classes were "attracted by the opportunities of long-distance and maritime trade, the rising value of urban real estate, the new public offices available in the expanding [cities], and the chances for advantageous marriages into rich commercial families."[24] However, in the city, nobles discovered that their relationship with the lower classes had changed. Men had opportunities for advancement regardless of social class; the manorial system did not exist in urban centers of growth and progress.

Distributing Wealth:
The Rising Middle Class

As the Renaissance spread from southern to northern Europe, major cities experienced rapid population growth. In 1500 the population of Venice reached approximately one hundred thousand; by 1600 London had reached the same size. Much of this growth was due to the migration of peasants from neighboring countrysides.

People moved from rural villages to cities in order to benefit from the increasing economic opportunities in urban areas. The transition from the Middle Ages to the Renaissance was marked by commercial and economic expansion, and by a shift from an agricultural to a merchant society.

Merchant Society

The Renaissance was marked by the emergence of a thriving middle class of craftsmen, who produced goods and commodities, and trader-merchants, who purchased, transported, distributed, and resold the goods for profit wherever demand was high. As these merchants became successful, they spent money on additional goods and services, thereby increasing the wealth of other middle-class professions. For example, lawyers profited from the high demand for experts who could handle business contracts.

In the fourteenth century, Italy and Flanders (present-day France, Belgium, and the Netherlands) had particularly strong merchant societies. The primary reason for this is geographic. Many Italian cities were Mediterranean or Adriatic ports, conveniently and strategically located to receive goods from North Africa, Russia, and the Orient and ship them to the rest of Europe. Similarly, Flanders, directly across the English Channel from England, could easily import English wool and distribute it as raw material or finished textiles throughout Europe.

Wool was an essential part of England's merchant economy. Many English ports and trade centers, including London, Boston, and

A well-dressed merchant oversees goods in port. Merchants imported most of their wares from Africa and the Orient and distributed them throughout Europe.

Bristol, were dependent on the revenue that wool brought in. Some towns, such as Lincoln, York, and Leicester, became centers of textile manufacturing as well as trade in raw wool. The same thing occurred in Flanders, where many Flemish towns became famous for their exquisite textile production.

The Slave Trade

Italian traders also transported wool from England, but their greatest profits were from buying and selling Oriental spices, luxury goods, and slaves. According to historian William Manchester, spices commanded such a high price that "a sack of pepper, cinnamon, ginger, or nutmeg was worth more than a seaman's life, and a shipment from Araby would include fragrant ambergris, musk, . . . silks, damasks, gold, Indian diamonds, [and] celonese pears.[25] As for slavery, one Italian noblewoman writing about Spain during the late 1600s commented: "People have a great number of slaves here, and they are bought and sold very dearly. They are Moors and Turks. Some of them are worth as much as four or five hundred ecus [old French coins]."[26]

In fact, the slave trade was such a lucrative business that Portugal's merchant society depended on it. By the fifteenth century the Portuguese were importing approximately one thousand slaves a year, most of them black, and by the mid–sixteenth century, about 3 percent of Portugal's population was black.

Many of these slaves were eventually traded to other countries, where they were highly prized. Historian John McKay describes the attitude with which many slaves were regarded:

In the late fifteenth century, [one Italian noblewoman] took pride in the fact that she had ten blacks, seven of them females; a black . . . maid was both a curiosity and a symbol of wealth. In 1491 Isabella of Este, duchess of Mantua, instructed her agent to secure a black girl between four and eight years old, "shapely and as black as possible." The duchess saw the child as a source of entertainment: "we shall make her very happy and shall have great fun with her." She hoped that the little girl would become "the best buffoon in the world."[27]

Slaves increased in value as peasants gained more rights. A slave could labor in the fields, be trained as a household servant, or perform a variety of other duties. For example, John Hale says: "Africans rowed gondolas for the Venetian employers, added a note of dusky exoticism to north Italian courts, and as servants were treated as pets (and lovers) in wealthy households throughout the northern Mediterranean."[28]

Extravagant Clothing

With wealth came enhanced social status, and newly affluent merchants soon sought the privileges and luxuries previously reserved for the nobility. For example, historian Philippe Erlanger quotes one Italian Renaissance man: "Merchants dress their wives like noblewomen, and allow themselves every pleasure, whatever the cost."[29]

Some of this clothing was quite extravagant; Erlanger offers this description of French garments:

Men and women wore sumptuous clothes of silks, brocades, cut velvets and lace; precious stones and gold nets on their hair. Materials streamed with silver and

A wealthy Renaissance woman dresses in extravagant attire. Because merchants could afford more luxuries, they emulated the lifestyle and appearance of the nobility.

the epitome of good style."[31] In Spain, upper- and middle-class men of the fifteenth and sixteenth centuries wore doublets made rigid by stuffing horsehair or whalebone and cardboard between outer and inner layers of fabric. They also wore short cloaks with high collars. On their legs they sported knitted hose, over which they pulled puffy, padded pantaloons. Their hats were tall and large.

Spanish women stiffened the bodices of their dresses with whalebone and wire, and their ground-length skirts were supported by hoops. Like men, they wore cloaks out of doors, but women's cloaks were full-length. Both men and women wore large white tulle ruffs around their necks.

Clothing Restrictions

Although fashion styles differed from country to country, all of Europe believed that clothing should reflect social status. William Manchester explains:

Clothing served as a kind of uniform. . . . Some raiment was stigmatic. Lepers were required to wear gray coats and red hats, the skirts of prostitutes had to be scarlet, public penitents wore white robes. . . . Establishing one's social identity was important. Each man knew his place, believed it had been foreordained in heaven, and was aware that what he wore must reflect it.[32]

Accordingly, a man's social position was immediately apparent from his clothing, not only by custom but by law. Most countries had statutes restricting what type of clothing a person could wear. For example, in most places, only those of noble birth could wear fur. Historian Margaret Ashton explains: "In most European countries sumptuary laws

were always vivid in colour. Warm, flesh-tinted cosmetics were applied freely. Servants, pages, lackeys and ushers were also clad gaudily, half red and half yellow, or half green and half white. The young noblemen had slashed sleeves, and puffed out breeches with scarlet or vivid yellow silk linings which showed through to heighten the effect.[30]

However, not all Europeans wore such colorful clothing. In fact, Erlanger reports that the majority of Europeans regarded Spanish dress, which was primarily black, "as

Skirting the Law

Renaissance laws forbade merchants from dressing like nobles. However, many people ignored these laws. In his book The House of Medici, *historian Christopher Hibbert quotes an Italian Renaissance official, who was in charge of policing these laws, as he reported his difficulties to one of his superiors.*

"In obedience to the orders you gave me, I went out to look for forbidden ornaments on the women and was met with arguments such as are not to be found in any book of laws. There was one woman with the edge of her hood fringed out in lace and twined round her head. My assistant said to her, 'What is your name? You have a hood with lace fringes.' But the woman removed the laced fringe which was attached to the hood with a pin, and said it was merely a wreath. Further along we met a woman with many buttons in front of her dress; and my assistant said to her, 'You are not allowed to wear buttons.' But she replied, 'These are not buttons. They are studs. Look, they have no loops, and there are no buttonholes.' Then my assistant, supposing he had caught a culprit at last, went up to the woman and said to her, 'You are wearing ermine.' And he took out his book to write down her name. 'You cannot take down my name,' the woman protested. 'This is not ermine. It is the fur of a suckling.' 'What do you mean, suckling?' 'A kind of animal.'"

dictated what could be worn by whom. They covered materials (with the aim of encouraging national industries) and the display of jewelry and colour (with the aim of preventing the lower classes from aping their betters)."[33]

Middle-Class Housing

But as merchants grew rich and powerful, they began to challenge such restrictions. They not only dressed in opulent clothing but built lavish houses, some of which rivaled the wealthiest nobleman's home. For example, William Manchester describes the typical prosperous Renaissance Italian merchant "whose home in the marketplace . . . rose five stories and was built with beams filled in with stucco, mortar, and laths. Storerooms were piled high with expensive Oriental rugs and containers of powdered spices; clerks at high desks pored over accounts."[36]

Merchants also began to put more thought and expense into the design of their homes. Margaret Ashton reports that during the Renaissance "houses came to be designed by professional architects, not by builders, which meant that for the first time plans, elevations, and sections had to be drawn in advance."[35]

Building materials differed throughout Europe, but once again reflected social status. For example, though in England many well-to-do merchants had houses of clay, in Spain only stone was suitable for the middle and upper classes. Therefore, when a group of sixteenth-century Spaniards visited England, they were astonished to see relatively wealthy people living in what they considered to be the housing of peasants. One of them later wrote: "These English have their houses made of sticks and dirt, but they fare commonly as well as their king."[36]

However, some customary building practices had to change as the expansion of cities created new problems. McKay explains that many European cities, particularly in the north, were surrounded by formidable medieval walls built to withstand sieges and considered permanent:

> Because space within the town walls was limited, expansion occurred upward. Second and third stories were built jutting out over the ground floor and thus over the street. Neighbors on the opposite side did the same. Since the streets were narrow to begin with, houses lacked fresh air and light. Initially, houses were made of wood and thatched with straw. Fire represented a constant danger, and because houses were built so close together, fires spread rapidly. Municipal governments consequently urged construction in stone or brick.[37]

Interestingly, the houses of the rich were not segregated from the rest of the community. Philippe Erlanger explains: "In the large towns there were not rich quarters and poor quarters, aristocratic and plebeian quarters. Social distances were too vast, too visible, too well recognized for there to be any need to mark them geographically."[38]

Poor Sanitation

Therefore, a rich man's house and a poor man's house often sat side by side, on city streets that were notoriously dirty. According to McKay, one cause of poor sanitation was rapid population growth:

> Most . . . cities developed haphazardly. There was little town planning. As the

A woodcut image of Venice, Italy, during the Renaissance. Bordered by the sea and crisscrossed by canals, the city was forced to build upward instead of outward.

population increased, space became more and more limited. Air and water pollution presented serious problems. Many families raised pigs for household consumption in sties next to the house. Horses and oxen, the chief means of transportation and power, dropped tons of dung on the streets every year.[39]

It was also common practice to dump human waste on the streets. According to historian Marzieh Gail:

> When there was a narrow space between two buildings, planks might be laid from wall to wall, making a precarious latrine into which the unwary sometimes fell. . . . In Edinburgh . . . [waste] receptacles were emptied out the window, early in the morning, with the warning cry: "Gardy-loo!" from the French *gare l'eau*, meaning *look out for the water*. The City Guard would later clean out the streets, except on the Sabbath.[40]

Many townspeople in the lower classes lived in unsanitary conditions within their homes as well. In crowded cities, large families shared small rooms, sometimes on a second floor above a shop or someone else's living quarters. Sometimes a kitchen was used as a bedroom, and all water had to come from fountains, wells, or other receptacles in public squares.

A Shortage of Manual Laborers

But as merchants brought more wealth into communities, living conditions improved. Philippe Erlanger reports that a merchant's paid servants often demanded more money from their wealthy employers and consequently "grew rich so fast that it became diffi-

cult to maintain the household,"[41] quitting household service as soon as savings permitted.

At this point, former servants would begin to dress and live like merchants, just as prosperous merchants wanted to dress and live like nobility. People became more materialistic and less willing to perform manual labor for low pay.

For example, in Italy, a strong merchant economy led to massive construction projects that required hundreds of laborers to complete. But as demand for workers grew, their salaries had to be increased to ensure their loyalty to a project. Consequently, according to Erlanger, "It was difficult to find recruits for humble jobs. In fact the money which they earned so rapidly in the workyards gave most workmen the ambition to become employers and middle-class citizens as fast as possible."[42]

Construction boomed during the Renaissance, and skilled craftsmen were in demand. These stonemasons—once considered peasant laborers—could now command higher wages and other privileges.

In A History of Private Life, *historian Alain Collomp explains that inns did not offer much privacy.*

"In boarding houses and inns many beds were often crowded into every room. [One Renaissance writer] praised the quality of German inns, some of which offered heated rooms with single beds and hallways allowing access without having to pass through other rooms. The Count de Forbin recounts in his *Memoirs* (1677) a night spent in an inn at Montargis: 'It was time to go to bed. They put all four of us in one room with three beds.' The other three were travelers whom the count had met on the road: a canon from Chartres . . . and two unknown 'gentlemen' wearing officers' uniforms, who turned out to be highway robbers, one of whom would later be executed . . . in Paris."

Other types of workers also earned enough to spend money on clothing, luxury goods, entertainment, and travel. For example, Erlanger says that "innkeepers and tavernkeepers grew rich thanks to the enormous influx of travellers. . . . So did the tailors, embroiderers, jewellers, and all the tradesmen connected with clothes, church linen and finery. The yardage of material sold every year was considerable."[43]

Marriage

Marriage was another way to get rich. Essentially, marriage was a business transaction; fathers chose husbands and wives for their children based on political and financial considerations. A middle-class girl could improve her social status by marrying an upper-class boy. At the same time, a son of nobility could improve his economic position by marrying a wealthy merchant's daughter, whose dowry, the money or goods a woman brought to marriage, was substantial. Without a dowry, usually provided by a bride's family, a Renaissance girl could not wed.

In some places, dowries were limited by government regulation. However, in unregulated areas, the total dowry could be so excessive that some families could not afford to pay it. Therefore, according to historian Margaret King: "Often a father was unwilling or unable to take on the task of providing a dowry for his daughter and she needed to provide one for herself."[44] Lower-class girls typically worked for years as household servants before they could afford to become wives.

Nonetheless, it was a necessary expense, because girls who did not marry by the age

Marriage was another means of climbing the social ladder in Renaissance Europe.

A 1612 collection of writings entitled The Essays or Counsels, Civil and Moral *by English author Sir Francis Bacon, reprinted in the* Norton Anthology of English Literature, *includes a section called* Of Marriage and Single Life.

Prominent English scholar Sir Francis Bacon examined the changing Renaissance society in his witty essays.

"He that hath wife and children hath given hostages to fortune, for they are impediments to great enterprises, either of virtue or mischief. Certainly the best works, and of greatest merit for the public, have proceeded from the unmarried or childless men, which both in affection and means have married and endowed the public. Yet it were great reason that those that have children should have greatest care of future times, unto which they know they must transmit their dearest pledges. . . . Unmarried men are best friends, best masters, best servants; but not always best subjects, for they are [likely] to run away. . . . Certainly, wife and children are a kind of discipline of humanity; and single men, though they be many times more charitable because their means are less [depleted], yet, on the other side, they are more cruel and hard-hearted . . . because their tenderness is not so oft called upon."

of twenty-one had no position in society. In fact, explains Margaret King: "Social life did not include a category for the unmarried woman outside of the religious life."[45] Without a husband, a young woman's place was in a convent. A widow was usually sent to live with her father or other male relative after her husband's death. However, in some places, the widow of a tradesman could take over his shop for a limited period of time while she looked for another husband. If her business was lucrative, she usually had many suitors.

The Power of the European Monarchs

As more people acquired wealth, the monarchs of Europe found ways to take some of it away. McKay explains: "The existence of wealth did not escape the attention of kings and other rulers. Wealth could be taxed, and through taxation kings could create strong and centralized states."[46] The monarchy was therefore strengthened during the Renaissance. Historian Henry Lucas explains:

Kings and princes no longer were forced to draw their incomes chiefly from [their own estates] but began to collect hard cash from their subjects. They built up a bureaucratic government, maintained armies of mercenaries [paid soldiers], and steadily drew into their hand governmental functions which in former ages had been controlled by [lesser nobility]. They were especially jealous of the rights to dispense justice. Thus . . . [by] controlling purse and sword, [they] became more powerful than ever.[47]

The new merchant economy therefore greatly benefited the monarchy system. At the same time, it lessened the power of the nobility, which was now competing with merchants for control of city governments.

Politics and Banking

As the Renaissance progressed, the wealthy middle classes became more influential in politics. In fact, many monarchs encouraged their participation in government, offering them high places in royal courts. The reason for this often had to do with money. Kings needed cash to finance foreign wars or maintain lavish courts, and many people in the rising middle class were in a position to lend it.

Led by wealthy merchant families, the banking industry flourished during the Renaissance, particularly in Italy. Lucas reports that prominent families "lent enormous sums to princes who had to finance wars. . . . They also financed the popes in their many undertakings such as crusades and wars in Naples and Sicily. . . . Borrowers usually paid exorbitant rates of interest or heavy bonuses and commissions. Lending of money became exceedingly profitable, and many fortunes were made."[48]

One of the wealthiest banking families in Italy was the Medici family. The heads of this family, particularly Cosimo (1389–1464) and Lorenzo (1449–1492) were also extremely powerful politicians. From 1434 to 1494, and again from 1512 to 1527, members of the Medici family ruled the city-state of Florence

Banking became a profitable business for already wealthy Renaissance merchants. Monarchies were always in need of money to finance wars and expeditions, and bankers were ready to lend large sums at high interest rates.

as virtual princes, and in 1530 they became its hereditary rulers, a position they held until 1734. Two Medicis eventually became popes.

Italian City-States

The concentration of so much political power in one family was not unusual, particularly in Italy. In 1422, Florence had a population of approximately forty thousand people, yet only six hundred men ruled the city. Similarly, Venice had a population of eighty-four thousand, but only two hundred men were in positions of influence. One reason for this was the political structure of the region, different from that of the rest of Europe.

Italy was divided into independently governed sections called city-states, typically consisting of one large city that dominated neighboring towns and countryside. City-

states evolved during the twelfth century, when associations of freemen, primarily merchants, established political and economic independence from the country's nobility. Over time, the power of these merchants became as absolute as the authority of the nobles had been. John McKay reports that "by 1300 signori (despots, or one-man rulers) or oligarchies (the rule of merchant aristocracies) had triumphed everywhere."[49]

Merchant aristocracies maintained political power through labor organizations called guilds. For example, in Florence, only guild members could serve on the primary governing body, called the Signoria. The Signoria consisted of nine men, or priori, whose two-month term of service was compensated by a small salary and an elaborately decorated crimson coat. In addition, the men of the Signoria had to live together in luxurious quarters in the Palazzo della Signoria.

Elections were held in what appeared to be a democratic way. Names of eligible men were put in leather bags called borse and then drawn at random. However, historian Christopher Hibbert explains that in reality, this system was not democratic at all, because only guild members could participate. Moreover, the selection process quickly became corrupt:

> [The election] was controlled by a few of the richest merchant families who contrived to ensure that only the names of reliable supporters found their way into the borse, or, when this proved impossible, that a [special meeting be called] . . . to "reform" the borse, thus disposing of any unreliable Priori who might have been elected to the Signoria. In fact, it was a government carried on mainly by the rich and almost exclusively in their interests.[50]

Dancing

"We find her dancing frequently except when an ulcer above her ankle made her limp. The Spaniards complained that the English idea of a dance was simply to jump in the air; but Elizabeth went on with her leaping. Six or seven [dances] a morning, apart from music and singing, was her daily exercise; so we are told, in 1589. (The Earl of Oxford . . . remarked, 'By the blood of God, she had the worst of voyce, and did everything with the worst grace that ever any woman did.') Near the end, almost seventy years old, she is glimpsed 'dancing the Spanish Panic [a type of dance] to a whistle and a tabourer, none other being with her by my Lady Warwick.' She liked music too. When she hunted at Bushey Park—that is, when beasts were herded into enclosures and chased out in front of pavilions to be slaughtered—she had musicians hidden in bowers of greenery while a lady disguised as a nymph made a curtsey and offered a crossbow to the Queen."

Queen Elizabeth I of England reigned from 1558 to 1603.

Guilds

Not everyone who wanted to belong to a guild was allowed to join one. Each guild was an arm of a particular profession—law, banking, wool manufacture, or baking, for example—and had its own requirements for admission. For example, many guilds denied membership to anyone who could not read. Apprenticeships were limited, too, according to William Manchester: "The sons of master journeymen [craftsmen] were given special consideration; property qualifications were imposed on outsiders, and the children of peasants and laborers were excluded."[51]

In the republic of Florence, there were twenty-one guilds, seven major and fourteen minor. The seven major guilds, in order of prestige, were: the lawyers guild; the wool merchants guild; the silk merchants guild; the cloth merchants guild; the bankers guild; the guild of doctors, apothecaries, shopkeepers, merchants selling spices and dyes, and artists and craftsmen who used dyes; and the guild of merchants and craftsmen who bought or used animal skins and furs. The minor guilds

Many people in Europe thought that the English led easier lives than people elsewhere. In The Age of Courts and Kings, *Philippe Erlanger quotes a Dutchman writing in 1575 who offers this description of the lifestyle of Englishwomen.*

"Although the women there are entirely in the power of their husbands, except for their lives, yet they are not so strictly kept as they are in Spain or elsewhere. Nor are they shut up: but they have the free management of the house or house-keeping, after the fashion of those of the Netherlands, and others of their neighbours. They go to market to buy what they like best to eat. They are well dressed, fond of taking it easy, and commonly leave the care of household matters and drudgery to their servants. They sit before their doors, decked out in fine clothes, in order to see and be seen by the passers-by. In all banquets and feasts they are shown the greatest honour; they are placed at the upper end of the table, where they are first served. . . .

All the rest of the time they employ in walking and riding, in playing at cards or otherwise, in visiting their friends and keeping company, conversing with their equals (whom they term gossips) and their neighbours, and making all this with the permission and knowledge of their husbands, as such is the custom. Although the husbands often recommend to them the pains, industry and care of the German or Dutch women, who do what the men ought to do both in the house and in the shops, for which services in England men are employed, nevertheless the women usually persist in retaining their customs. This is why England is called the Paradise of married women. The girls who are not yet married are kept much more rigorously and strictly than in [other countries]."

were those of simple tradesmen such as tailors, cooks, butchers, leatherworkers, stonemasons, and innkeepers.

Members of the major guilds looked down on members of the minor ones. In turn, members of the minor guilds looked down on those who could not belong to a guild. According to Hibbert, these included "tens of thousands of those ordinary workers in the wool and silk trades, the weavers, spinners and dyers, the combers and beaters who, like carters and boatmen, labourers, pedlars and all those who had no permanent workshop, did not belong to a guild at all and—though they constituted more than three-quarters of the population of the city—were not allowed to form one." [52]

John Hale reports that guilds had not only "concern for the training of craftsmen [and] regulation of quality" but "a rigidly policed method of entry [into their occupations] from a labour force which was growing at a disturbing rate." [53] In other words, guilds did not want too many members, because then the value of each individual worker would decline. This was one way of ensuring middle-class prosperity.

Other cities in Italy also used the guild system to increase the wealth of their merchants. The number of these guilds varied from city to city, and even within a single city the number of guilds could change over the years as new trade categories and divisions were created. For example, in Venice the shoemakers guild was eventually divided into those who made high-quality shoes for nobles and those who made clogs for ordinary citizens. In Rome, the number of guilds grew from eighteen in 1400 to thirty-two in 1500 to fifty-five in 1600.

Eventually, merchants in other countries realized the benefits of the guild system, and it began to spread throughout Europe. However, Florence was one of the few places to allow its guilds so much control over govern-ment. In England, for instance, where the no-bility wielded more influence, the guilds con-fined themselves primarily to business issues, enforcing rigid regulations to maintain the quality of craftsmanship. Marzieh Gail offers several examples:

> To maintain the quality of pewter, which was often cheapened, the maker had to stamp his name on each piece. The price of food was regulated in order to keep the cost of living down. Wool-beaters could not work at night. Because of the drinking and carousing, inns were not allowed close to churches. All this was good, but the total effect of so many regulations was to put a brake on the ambitious. If, for ex-ample, you sold old clothes you could not also sell new coats.[54]

The Influence of Guilds

Guilds throughout Europe also performed many important functions in the community. They helped sick workers pay for medical care, and they provided financial assistance to widows and orphans. They sponsored various community projects and entertainments and took part in public parades and processions. They also tried to improve public health, by regulating such practices as the slaughter of animals.

In addition, their literacy requirements created a greater demand for reading and mathematical skills among those who wanted to succeed. In this way, members of the mid-dle class became not only more wealthy but more educated. Eventually, their financial rise was accompanied by a cultural elevation, as they became interested in literature and new ideas.

These skilled furriers were probably members of a local guild. Their membership would have ensured that their products were of good quality.

The Power of Knowledge: Education and Humanism

As Renaissance society increasingly depended on trade and commerce, new business practices were established. For example, merchants developed the concept of credit to facilitate the management and transfer of large sums of money, particularly in dealing with distant countries. Renaissance accountants invented double-entry bookkeeping, in which every transaction is entered in both a credit and a debit account, to assure balanced books and make possible more sophisticated analysis of the true costs and profits of a business.

The Importance of Math and Law

However, at the beginning of the Renaissance, many people were poor at math. According to John Hale, even literate men "were seldom able to do more than add and subtract, double and halve." Most people could not perform computations with fractions, nor did they learn the multiplication table. Moreover, Hale reports, "Addition and subtraction were hampered by being carried out from left to right. There were . . . at least eight methods of multiplication, even more of subtraction." [55]

This lack of proficiency in math was not a handicap during the Middle Ages, when bookkeeping primarily involved only simple transactions between landlord and tenants. However, in a merchant economy, mathematical skills were vital. Businessmen needed

An upper-class woman educates her son. Such practices increased the literacy of Renaissance children and of the mothers who often served as their teachers.

skilled accountants, and because they were rare, bookkeepers were typically well paid.

Likewise, merchants as well as government officials and royalty valued lawyers who knew contract law. In fact, Lucas reports that most kings considered lawyers to be "more loyal servants of the crown and more efficient administrators than the sons of the nobility." [56] Therefore, "mastery of this law proved a sure road to a profitable career, and fathers solicitous for their sons' welfare introduced them to its study." [57]

Literacy

Literacy was valued less for its own sake than as a necessary business skill. Businessmen needed to know how to read contracts and write orders, and the most powerful guilds had the strictest literacy requirements. For this reason, the middle class encouraged the establishment of more and more grammar schools in European cities, and eventually two to three times more urban dwellers than rural folk could read and write. Hale says:

Peasants' sons who did go to school and showed promise there were likely to leave the country for . . . town life. Men of substance in the country could commonly read and write and keep accounts . . . [but] the proportion of those who could read and write in the town was much higher; . . . something like sixty per cent of Londoners could, and in a city like Florence the proportion may have been higher still."[58]

In addition, because people valued literacy primarily as a way to succeed in business, women had far lower literacy rates than men, and a man's ability to read and write often depended upon his profession. For example, historian Roger Chartier reports that by the late Renaissance in England

Nearly all clerics, notables, and important merchants knew how to write. Skilled artisans (goldsmiths, harness-makers, drapers) and yeomen could write in seven or eight out of ten cases. In most other

Student Diversions

In Renaissance England, many students enjoyed playing a game similar to football, but much more violent; many English critics felt it brought too much discord into society. Philippe Erlanger, in The Age of Courts and Kings, *quotes one such critic, who wrote about football in 1583.*

"I protest unto you that it may rather be called a friendly kind of fight, than a play or recreation; a bloody and murdering practice, than a fellowly sport or pastime. For doth not every one lie in a wait for his adversary, seeking to overthrow him and to pick him on his nose, though it be upon hard stones, in ditch or dale, in valley or hill, or what place soever it be he careth not, so he have him down. And he that can serve the most of this fashion, he is counted the only fellow, and who but he? So that by this means, sometimes their necks are broken, sometimes their backs, sometimes their legs, sometime their arms, sometime one part thrust out of joint, sometime another, sometimes their noses gush out with blood, sometimes their eyes start out, and sometimes hurt in one place, sometimes in another. . . . They have sleights to meet one betwixt two, to dash him against the heart with their elbows, to hit him under the short ribs with their gripped fists, and with their knees to catch him upon the hip, and to pick him on his neck, with an hundred such murdering devices. And hereof groweth envy, malice, rancour, choler, hatred, displeasure, enmity, and what not else; and sometimes fighting, brawling, contention, quarrel picking, murder, homicide, and great effusion of blood, as esperience daily teacheth."

trades, especially textiles and clothing, only about one in two could sign their names. Next came the village artisans and merchants (blacksmiths, carpenters, millers, butchers, and so forth), of whom only 30 to 40 percent could sign. At the bottom of the scale were building laborers, fishermen, shepherds, husbandmen, and agricultural workers, of whom at most one in four could sign their names.[59]

The Quality of Education

However, reading words is not the same as understanding them, and many technically literate people had only the most superficial concept of literature. For example, Hale says: "The clergy . . . could all, in theory at least, read and write and had been trained to study. . . . [But] reports on monasteries . . . suggest that especially in rural areas there were many priests and monks who were too ignorant to understand the services they read, too uncertainly literate to have their minds extended by reading."[60]

One reason for this limitation was the generally poor quality of instruction. In most European cities, any knowledgeable man could proclaim himself a teacher, no matter how capable a teacher he actually was. In rural communities, instructors were often barely literate men and women who worked for little money or in exchange for farm produce. Some were private tutors, working for only one family, while others taught grammar school to the children of several families in a village.

Much of this instruction was conducted in the teachers' native French, German, or Italian, languages considered common, or vulgar, and therefore inferior to Latin. Latin was the language of success; it was the primary form of discourse among the upper

An engraving from 1453 portrays the one hundred clerks of New College, a religious institution in Oxford, England. Because the clergy had access to church libraries and were often well educated, they were considered ideal teachers and tutors.

classes, and all business contracts were written in Latin. It was also the language of theologians. Every religious service in the Catholic Church was conducted in Latin.

And so the merchant aristocracies of Italian city-states eventually decided to regulate their schools, requiring that teachers knew Latin. Children seven to ten years old learned to read and write in Latin and studied logic, rhetoric, and poetry. Fourteen- to eighteen-year-olds also studied music, arithmetic, geometry, and astronomy.

Outside of Italian city-states, parents who wanted to make sure their children learned

Latin often sent them to religious schools. Boys went to country monasteries, either as day students or residents, where monks taught a variety of subjects. William Manchester explains:

> All teaching . . . was in Latin; younger monks and country youth were led through primary instruction in the *trivium*—grammar, rhetoric, and dialectics (the art of reasoning)—and bright students were encouraged to tackle the *quadrivium:* astronomy, arithmetic, geometry, and music.[61]

Girls attended school in Catholic convents, typically as residents but sometimes as day students. However, these schools were extremely expensive to attend for those not intending to join the convent. As a result, only daughters of

Students learned the basics of writing, speaking, and reasoning in Renaissance schools. Gifted students could also aspire to mathematics or music.

the wealthiest Europeans went to convent schools, where nuns read them Bible passages and taught them Latin, music, needlework, and manners. In France, some convent schools also offered girls instruction in composition, geography, and other advanced subjects, but such opportunities were rare. Nonetheless, scholar Joan Ferrante says, "religious schools produced virtually all the great intellectual women of the Middle Ages."[62]

The Catholic Church was not the only religious institution to provide boarding schools. In England, for example, there were fifteen Quaker boarding schools in 1671, two for girls and two for both boys and girls. However, according to historian Margaret King, "the goals of these schools were limited." They did not provide as thorough an education as Catholic schools, particularly for girls. King says that Quakers believed "girls were to be instructed so as to fulfill their domestic and religious duties, not so as to attain a general education."[63]

Humanism

Wealthy parents had other ways to ensure that their children received a good, Latin-based education. They could send their sons to secular boarding schools, prestigious and typically expensive institutions that taught a wide variety of subjects, including mathematics, composition, geography, history, Latin, Greek, French, German, and fencing. This choice was extremely popular among the upper classes in England during the 1500s. Another popular educational choice for wealthy students was the private tutor. Royal children always had tutors, and other noble children often joined them for group instruction at their royal residence.

Many of these private tutors, as well as the instructors at exclusive boarding schools, believed in an educational philosophy called humanism. According to Hale, humanists believed that "lessons were to shape the pupil's character and prepare him for a life of useful service." Studying grammar enabled a student to speak and write clearly on many themes and to many audiences, whereas studying history "would provide him with examples of behaviour to shun or follow." Similarly, humanists believed that morals should be taught "to stress the high standards of personal behaviour that were expected of the responsible citizen."[64]

Moreover, humanists placed less emphasis on rote memorization and more on insight and reasoning. Hale notes, for example, that the humanist teacher Marineo Siculo, who taught the noblemen of Spain in Queen Isabella's court, "pushed his students as quickly as possible through the rote-learning of grammatical rules to the texts themselves, to the personalities of their authors; in this way, he claimed, 'they will certainly advance more, and become not grammarians but Latinists.'"[65]

Among teachers who were not humanists, lessons were far more tedious. Students typically learned by copying and memorizing their lessons, and independent thinking was discouraged. Hale elaborates:

> With a few . . . exceptions the emphasis was on learning by rote from antiquated schoolbooks, some of them copied and printed unchanged from the twelfth and thirteenth centuries. Such books—Latin grammars for the most part—were read aloud and copied down sentence by sentence by the pupils, the metrical form into which many of them were cast emphasising the stress on mere memory training.[66]

Classical Manuscripts

In addition to new teaching methods, humanists introduced new ideas based on ancient models into the Renaissance world. Humanists were so named because they believed that it was important to study human thoughts and achievements from a historical perspective. They therefore became interested in old texts and unearthed classical Greek and Latin manuscripts. Sarah Howarth explains:

> The great interest in Greek and Latin books led to people discovering ancient works that had lain neglected for centuries. Some were found in monasteries, like a work by the Roman politician and writer Cicero, which was discovered by an

Bad Behavior

University students did not always behave well. In The Age of Courts and Kings, *historian Philippe Erlanger reports that public behavior became so bad in England that in 1571 the vice-chancellor of Cambridge University issued an order that no student could go swimming in any local stream or pool. Nonetheless, the situation did not improve, and Erlanger quotes one English scholar's complaint.*

"Gentlemen or rich men's sons often bring the Universities into much slander. For, standing upon their reputation and liberty, they ruffle and roist it out, exceeding in apparel, and riotous company which draweth them from their books unto another trade. And for excuse, when they are charged with breach of good order, think it sufficient to say they are gentlemen, which grieveth many not a little."

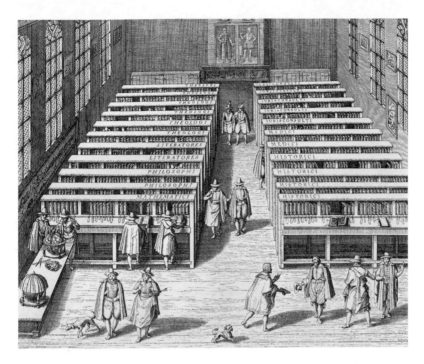

Few libraries existed in Europe at the beginning of the Renaissance because of the limited supply of hand-copied books. When the printing press accelerated book production, more libraries emerged.

Italian "in a pile of wastepaper." This was not his only finding. Having traveled to Germany to attend a great Church council, he spent some time "searching through the monasteries there for some of the books in Latin that had been forgotten." When he went home, he carried with him books of poetry and works on science, medicine, and many other subjects."[67]

In this way, humanists reintroduced classical thought into Renaissance education. According to historian Louis B. Wright, this "brought new intellectual vitality" to society as people began to believe "that the great minds of antiquity had much to teach them."[68]

Many important people of the period supported this revival of learning. Renaissance writer Leonardo Bruni (1370–1444) describes one wealthy merchant, Palla Strozzi, who "never wasted time by loitering, but returned home after business and spent his time in studying Greek and Latin. Being greatly devoted to letters, he bought a fine collection of books which he housed in a handsome building in Santa Trinita for the use of the public."[69]

The first public library was established in Florence, Italy, by the Medici family in 1440. Housed within the monastery of San Marco, it was 180 feet long and 36 feet wide, with shelves made of cypress wood. According to Howarth, within a few years similar libraries appeared in England and Hungary as well as throughout Italy: "Libraries were founded by clergymen, . . . by princes and powerful individuals . . . , and by private citizens. They were places that were intended for study. Today libraries lend out their books, but at this time, books were so valuable that they were often chained down to stop people from stealing them."[70]

Books were valuable because they were scarce, and they were scarce because until the fifteenth century they had to be copied by hand. However, in approximately 1455, an

Gutenberg's printing press could produce uniform duplicates of texts in far less time than it took to hand copy them. The ease of printing also increased the variety of texts that were distributed.

important invention appeared: the movable-type printing press, most often credited to German inventor Johannes Gutenberg. Previously, only money and playing cards had been mass-produced, their printed impressions made by inking groups of words and pictures carved on wooden blocks. But with movable-type printing, single letters were carved on small, reusable blocks that could be moved around in any arrangement to form individual words. This meant that it was relatively easy to create multiple, uniform copies of any book.

With the invention of the printing press, more people had access to books. Hale reports: "By the end of the fifteenth century the number of books printed has been estimated at six million, composed of about thirty thousand different titles produced by something like one thousand different printers."[71]

For the first time, some of these books were intended for common people. One of the earliest and most widely distributed books was the Bible, printed in the vernacular, or common, languages. Other religious materials, such as prayer booklets, were also popular, as were political pamphlets and practical manuals of medicine and housekeeping. However, the most sought-after books were for the middle and upper classes. They were copies of classical Greek and Latin manuscripts, often annotated with comments by humanist scholars. Hale reports:

> The printing press made the labours of classical scholars more and more conspicuous in booksellers' shops. Phrase books and compilations of quotations, like Erasmus's *The Abundance of Words and Ideas* of 1512 and his enormously popular *Adages*, reissued in one edition after another, assumed that the educated writer would want to pepper his writings with classical tags and allusions.[72]

Knowing classical phrases became a sign of cleverness. Therefore, according to McKay,

"Literary humanists of the fourteenth century wrote each other highly stylized letters imitating ancient authors, and they held witty philosophical dialogues in conscious imitation of [ancient scholars]."[73]

In fact, anything related to ancient times was considered a mark of quality. People began searching for ancient Roman coins and other portable artifacts, sometimes desecrating or damaging ancient ruins to find them. They also grew excited over archaeological studies of ancient sites. For example, Wright says, "When bones purported to be those of the Roman historian Livy were unearthed in Padua in 1413, a thrill ran through Italy like that in America when men landed on the moon."[74]

As merchants and scholars shared their classical interests with people from other countries, fascination with ancient texts spread. By the end of the fifteenth century, students from France, Germany, England, and the Netherlands were traveling to Italy to study original Latin texts. According to McKay, these traveling scholars then carried their knowledge home, where they "interpreted Italian ideas about and attitudes toward classical antiquity . . . in terms of their own traditions."[75]

Spreading Humanism Through Universities

Universities also fostered the spread of classical studies. By the fifteenth century, there were approximately eighty universities in Europe. Each was unique, having developed within a particular social and political setting. According to scholar Ernst Breisach:

> The quality of education varied from university to university as did the prestige of these institutions. During the fourteenth and fifteenth centuries theology was preeminent at the University of Paris. . . . For the study of medicine a student was better advised to go to Montpellier in southern France. As for law, Bologna reigned supreme, with Padua occupying a respectable place.[76]

Many students therefore moved from university to university, changing locations as they changed subjects they wished to study. This fostered the dispersion of ideas throughout Europe. However, it also limited the kind of education a lower-class person could get. As John Hale points out, the fact that it "was frequently necessary to travel far" to get the best education "probably weighted the scales against the poor student who could not afford to travel."[77]

Rigid Schoolmasters

Country schoolmasters were sometimes stern, forbidding figures. Erlanger's The Age of Courts and Kings *offers one description of such a man, written in 1632.*

"He looks over his scholars with as great and grave a countenance as the emperor over his army. He will not at first be over busy to examine his usher [assistant schoolteacher], for fear he should prove, as many curates [assistant clergymen], better scholars than the chief master. As he sits in his seat, he must with a grace turn his moustachios up; his sceptre lies not far from him, the rod; he uses martial law most, and the day of execution ordinarily is Friday: at six o'clock his army all begin to march; at seven they keep rendezvous, and at five or six at night they take up their quarters."

Hale notes that most university students were not poor in the first place. Only 9 percent of students at the University of Leipzig, Germany, needed financial aid to help pay for lecture fees and room and board. Most students had wealthy middle- or upper-class parents who wanted them to succeed in business, politics, or law. Some of these students also brought private tutors and personal valets with them to the university. They lived in rented palaces or other luxurious homes, whereas poor students typically lived in cheap boarding houses.

Few students were younger than eighteen, and all were men. Classes could be large or small, depending on the size of the univer-sity; the largest schools enrolled approximately a thousand students. Most universities held classes from 6 A.M. to 5 P.M., with a break at 10 A.M. for lunch, and most classes followed a prescribed form: Instructors read standard lectures aloud and, according to Hale, "spontaneity . . . was frowned upon."[78] Moreover, Hale says, "Greater emphasis was laid on memory and argument than on originality or the development of critical ability."[79] He explains that the aim of the universities was "a training of the mind which would be useful in a variety of avocations; they existed to turn out experts."[80]

Just as at the grammar-school level, parental pressure motivated this emphasis on

Lawyers Criticized

A client solicits the services of a lawyer. Legal aid was not cheap during the Renaissance, and bribery was sometimes needed to persuade a lawyer to handle a case.

According to J. R. Hale, in his book Renaissance Europe, *"Jurisprudence, like medicine, was a subject of the highest prestige. . . . A legal profession . . . was a passport to promotion in the administrative or diplomatic services of both church and state." However, lawyers were not well liked within society.*

"Already a tradition, abuse of the lawyers grew in volume and bitterness. . . . And over and above their normal charges lawyers were universally accused of taking bribes. To have an appetite 'as indiscriminate as a lawyer's wallet' was already a proverbial expression in France. What is the most delicate thing in the world? A lawyer's shoulder: if you do but touch it his hand shoots out for money. In a multitude of expressions like this literature expressed society's distrust."

A typical student during the Renaissance would be trained in memorization and logic. Critical thinking skills were often overlooked because they were considered unnecessary to succeed in business.

practical skills. Fathers wanted their sons to learn practical skills that would help them succeed in the new merchant society. Nonetheless, as humanist ideas were carried from university to university, some instructors developed a different approach. Howarth explains why:

> The way that the ancient Greeks and Romans studied the world was completely different from the approach taken by scholars in the Middle Ages. The Greeks and Romans had studied scientific subjects, making experiments and recording their observations. With the coming of Christianity, these subjects and this approach had seemed less important, and so Greek and Roman methods were no longer used.[81]

During the Middle Ages, the church emphasized that the Bible was the source of all knowledge; it discouraged people from asking questions, scientific or otherwise, about the nature of the world and mankind. But just as the church's teachings about self-sacrifice and humility were ignored by the newly wealthy middle class, so too was its rigid thinking. As people learned classical ideas, they began to wonder about a great many things, and eventually to challenge church leaders, who were losing their influence over the educated and powerful merchants of Renaissance society.

Struggling to Maintain Control: The Church in Daily Life

As the middle class gained wealth and education, Renaissance society grew less spiritual and more materialistic. This attitude eventually was reflected in the Catholic Church. Increasingly, a variety of religious practices seemed designed to accumulate wealth and property rather than strengthen spiritual values. As historian Malcolm Vale points out: "In a society which was developing a profit economy, . . . the carrying out of Christ's injunctions . . . concerning [the desirability of] poverty was more difficult to implement."[82]

Missals and Indulgences

Christianity had been the dominant religion in Europe for a thousand years, hugely influential at all levels of society. Kings and commoners alike were subject to the supreme moral and spiritual authority of the church, centered in the pope in Rome. Legions of the faithful supported its activities, from housing local clergy to conducting massive crusades, all of which required a constant flow of funds. Renaissance clergymen found new ways to increase the wealth of the church. They had always received donations from worshipers, but not enough to pay for increasingly lavish and corrupt lifestyles. At all levels of the church hierarchy, expenses typically exceeded income.

To increase revenues, church officials first began to sell booklets called missals, which were written in both Latin and French. Missals reproduced church services, so worshipers could use them to recite prayers along with the priests. However, historian Francois Lebrun believes that few people actually used them, due to illiteracy and lack of interest:

> Even among the minority who knew how to read . . . probably only a small number owned and used missals and books of spiritual exercises. . . . In fact, apart from private use of missals [for personal prayer], which remained rare (except possibly in some urban parishes and in the chapels of religious communities open to laypersons), all attempts to involve the congregation in the prayers . . . recited at the altar ended in failure.[83]

The church then came up with another way to increase income. It noted that in many places, governments allowed criminals to pay a fine instead of receiving punishment, and it decided to adapt this practice to religion. Anyone who believed he or she had committed a religious sin could buy the church's forgiveness for that sin. This forgiveness was called an indulgence.

Indulgences had always been granted by the church, but until the Renaissance they had never been sold. Instead they had to be earned through some physical task, such as spending time helping the less fortunate or making a pilgrimage to a holy place.

A papal commissioner (far left) collects payment for letters of indulgence at a German country fair. The church adopted the practice of selling indulgences to increase revenues.

Once the Catholic Church decided that indulgences could be bought, it became easy for people who could afford them to obtain forgiveness. A member of the local clergy, usually a friar, was charged with tracking down sinners, determining the price of a sin, and exacting payment for it in exchange for an indulgence. The friar then deducted a commission for his trouble before sending the funds on to church leaders in Rome. William Manchester reports: "In Rome the contributions were welcomed and, in the beginning, used to finance hospitals, cathedrals, and crusades. Then other, less admirable causes appeared."[84] Many of these causes related to the personal needs of a series of corrupt popes, who lived in a particularly grand and dissipated fashion.

Church Corruption

As the clergy became more interested in riches than in spirituality, corruption and immoral behavior grew increasingly common. Many ignored their vows of temperance and celibacy. They also raided church coffers to pay for personal luxuries or to support their illegitimate children.

William Manchester says that even the humblest parish priests, many of whom came from the peasant class, soon "became indistinguishable from the nobility."[85] Philippe Erlanger quotes an Englishman writing in 1576 that one rector "wolde have taken away a mans wife from him by the high waie and used such filthy speech that they banished him out of their company." This same writer says that a local vicar "beat his wife in the churchyard, and is a common sower of discord amongst his neighbours; and he has two wives."[86]

Nepotism in church appointments was also a common occurrence, particularly at the highest levels of the Roman Catholic Church. For example, Pope Sixtus IV, who led the church from 1471 to 1484, named as cardinals five nephews and a grandnephew. He also appointed as archbishops two boys, ages eight and eleven, whom he liked but who had never received any religious instruction.

High-ranking religious leaders often appointed friends or relatives to other positions of power within the church. This bishop may have been ordained through such nepotism.

Pope Innocent VIII, who succeeded Sixtus, continued this practice. He named as cardinal his illegitimate son's fourteen-year-old brother-in-law, who would become Pope Leo X in 1513.

A New Religion

As a result of widespread corruption and excess among the clergy, many people called for the reformation of the church. Criticism came from all levels of Renaissance society. According to Ernst Breisach: "Condemnation of the clergy was a favorite pastime of peasants who considered the clergy's style of life to

be too comfortable, of town dwellers who found the 'unproductive' clergy too numerous in their cities, and of the better and better educated laymen who found many clergymen just not educated enough."[87]

One man who was particularly disturbed by the state of the church was Martin Luther. The son of a German peasant, Luther was a former Augustinian monk who taught theology at the university at Wittenberg. From studying the Bible, he came to believe that God's forgiveness could not be bought with money, that faith and not acts was the key to salvation. Therefore he grew angry when, in 1517, Pope Leo X began selling a large amount of indulgences to raise money for a monumental church, St. Peter's Basilica in Rome.

A procession of clergy passes in review for an emperor. Many clergy members were part of European courts, holding vast political as well as spiritual power.

Enraged by the corruption within the Catholic Church, Martin Luther wrote a list of the abuses and nailed them to the door of a church in Wittenberg. His protest fostered a religious schism that gave birth to the Protestant faith.

Luther wrote a document challenging this and several other Catholic practices, and then nailed it to the door of the church in Wittenberg. Later he began circulating copies of this document, called the Ninety-five Theses, to friends. One of them gave the work to a printer, who duplicated it and thereby spread Luther's call for reformation throughout Europe.

The result was a schism within the Roman Catholic Church and the consequent emergence of a new religious tradition, Protestantism. The name Protestant was taken from the word *protest*, which during the Renaissance meant "to stand for something" rather than "to oppose." The first Protestant religion was Lutheranism, but eventually other sects developed. For example, Calvinism was established in Geneva, Switzerland, by John Calvin, who had heard and modified Luther's teachings.

The main difference between Protestantism and Catholicism involves the relationship between God and the individual. Catholics believe that the pope speaks for God; his commandments are divinely inspired and therefore infallible. They also believe that God cannot hear prayer unless it is directed to him by the clergy. In contrast, Protestants reject the idea that one man can hold divine authority over the hearts, minds, and money of the people. They reject the necessity of the clergy's intervention for them before God. Instead they believe that God listens to every person, rich or poor, through private prayer. Therefore, Francois Lebrun says,

> The Protestant Reformation placed each believer in a direct relation with God and enjoined the faithful to read and question the Bible every day, since it contained the word of God. . . . All intermediaries other than the Book were either eliminated or minimized. . . . Hence not only were all Christians priests, equal by baptism, but most of the communal forms of piety maintained and encouraged by the Roman Catholic Church no longer had any reason to exist.[88]

Catholic Worship

One of these "communal forms of piety" was the celebration of the Mass, a worship service Catholics were required to attend every Sunday and on designated holy days. Although Mass was a group gathering, it did not require much participation on the part of those attending. According to Lebrun:

> Mass, though a collective rite, was for a long time less a communal devotion than a conjunction of individual prayers. . . . [The] faithful formed a passive audience, many of whom could not even see what was going on at the altar because they were seated in a side chapel or behind a . . . screen. . . . Catholics were exhorted to pass the time as devoutly as possible by reciting [private prayers].[89]

The important thing was to be praying in the presence of a priest. Worshipers paid little attention to his actions until he began his sermon. Then they tried to listen attentively. One Renaissance priest described the sermon as a "familiar explanation of the gospel of the day or of some point of Christian ethics for the instruction and edification of the congregation."[90]

The sermon was immediately preceded by a standard set of prayers for such prominent figures as the pope and the monarch; these prayers were spoken aloud by the entire congregation, which then listened to the priest's

Religious Restrictions

Catholics had to follow many church rules, one of which was that they could not eat meat on Fridays. This sometimes caused problems. In his book The Renaissance and the Reformation, *Henry Lucas quotes this sixteenth-century account of what happened when a man found a chick in an egg he was eating at a local tavern.*

"This I showed to a comrade; whereupon quoth he to me, 'Eat it up speedily, before the taverner see it, for if he mark it, you will have to pay . . . [extra money] for a fowl.' . . . In a trice I gulped down the egg, chicken and all. And then I remembered that it was Friday! Whereupon I said to my crony, 'You have made me commit a mortal sin, in eating flesh on the sixth day of the week!' But he averred that it was not a mortal sin . . . , seeing that such a chickling is accounted merely as an egg, until it is born. He told me, too, that it is just the same in the case of cheese in which there are sometimes grubs, as there are in cherries, peas, and new beans; yet all these may be eaten on Fridays. . . . But taverners are such rascals that they call them flesh to get more money."

reminders about church commandments. The sermon was followed by notices of upcoming religious events as well as the reading of marriage proclamations or episcopal letters.

Rituals and Ceremonies

In addition to attending Mass on Sundays, people participated in Catholic ceremonies at important times in their lives. For example, when a child was born, he or she was immediately received into the Catholic Church in the rite of baptism. During this ceremony, a priest anointed the newborn baby with water, symbolically washing away its sins and purifying its soul. The baptized child was then assigned godparents, who helped guide him or her in learning church teachings and obligations.

Children also learned church teachings in catechism class. When they graduated from this class, typically at age twelve, thirteen, or fourteen, they were eligible to participate in the rite of Holy Communion with their parents. The church required all Catholics to take communion once a year, at Easter. During communion, worshipers ate bread and sipped wine, which were symbolic of the Last Supper of Christ and represented the body and blood of Jesus.

Commemorating the resurrection of Christ, Easter was one of the most important events in the Catholic Church. Lebrun says: "Few people failed to observe this essential obligation of the faith. Those who refused were officially denounced as public sinners; if they persisted unto death, they were buried outside the consecrated ground of the cemetery."[91]

This annual ceremony was preceded by confession, a ritual during which worshipers examined and confessed their faults. During the Renaissance it was a communal ritual; people recited sins and requests for forgive-

Family and friends draw near as a priest prepares to baptize an infant in this Renaissance woodcut. Baptism remains an important ceremony in the Catholic Church.

ness out loud during Mass. Today Catholics confess their sins privately to a priest.

Confession also occurred at the end of life. On their deathbeds, Catholics called for a priest, to whom they would confess and repent their sins. They believed that unless they received final communion and the priest's blessing, they would have a difficult time entering heaven and might even end up in hell. It was a calamity to die before a priest could be found. Lebrun says:

Whereas many Catholics seem to have resented the obligation to confess annually, they looked upon the priest's presence at

A dying man confesses his sins to a Catholic priest. This last communion, in which the dying person repented for his or her lifetime of sins, was considered essential for entrance into heaven.

the deathbed as a grace and a necessity, and upon his absence as the worst of misfortunes. . . . Of all the obligations incumbent on Catholics, baptism and last rites were . . . looked upon . . . as necessities, the stakes being eternal salvation. Both birth and death were wrapped in ritual expressing the idea that no one can hope to achieve salvation on his own.[92]

Protestant Worship Practices

Protestants believe that anyone can achieve salvation on his or her own, so their rituals are very different from Catholic ones. There is no deathbed confession, for example, nor any other special rite for the dying. There are also no confessions during church services.

During the Renaissance, church attendance on Sundays was mandatory among Protestants. Protestant services included prayers, singing, Bible reading, an instructive sermon, and an occasional baptism; communion occurred four times a year. These services were conducted by the clergy. Even though Protestant leaders believed that people did not need someone to intervene with them before God, they still felt that some guidance was needed in order to keep services disciplined. Each parish therefore had a pastor or minister, who was helped in his duties by one or more schoolmasters and a group of elders.

Protestants were also encouraged to worship at home during the week. Many people therefore read the Bible daily, typically aloud with family members, in a morning and evening session during which they also sang psalms and said prayers.

Protestants also had to follow certain rules, which were harsher in some countries than in others. In the city of Geneva, for example, John Calvin controlled the members of his religion with extreme strictness. According to Manchester, Calvin "represented the ultimate in repression." Geneva was "a police state, ruled by . . . five pastors and twelve lay elders, with . . . [John Calvin] the dictator looming over all. . . . He was humorless and short-tempered. The slightest criticism enraged him. Those who questioned his theology he called 'pigs,' . . . 'dogs,' 'idiots,' and 'stinking beasts.'"[93]

Manchester lists some of what was forbidden to Calvinists:

dancing, singing, pictures, statues, relics, church bells, organs, altar candles; "inde-cent or irreligious" songs, staging or attending theatrical plays; wearing rouge, jewelry, lace, or "immodest" dress; speaking disrespectfully of your betters; extravagant entertainment; swearing, gambling, playing cards, hunting, drunkenness; naming children after anyone but figures in the Old Testament; reading "immoral or irreligious" books; and sexual intercourse, except between partners . . . who were married to one another.[94]

The punishment for offenses was severe. For example, according to Manchester:

A father who stubbornly insisted upon calling his newborn son Claude spent four days . . . in jail; so did a woman convicted of wearing her hair at an "immoral" height. A child who struck his parents was

Insincere Worship

In the late Renaissance, the Catholic Church instituted the private confession, whereby people could whisper their sins privately to a priest rather than aloud in a public ceremony. Many people took advantage of the private confession; however, the sincerity of their guilt and regret were sometimes questionable. In A History of Private Life, *Francois Lebrun quotes Christopher Sauvageon, a prior writing in 1700.*

"There is an entrenched but deplorable custom in this parish of going to confession without the slightest preparation. People approach the confessional without having examined their consciences in any way. They rush to church, hasten to the confessional, and practically fight one another to be the first to enter. But once at the priest's feet . . . they almost never remember when they made their last confession. Most of them have not completed their last penance. They have done nothing and accuse themselves of nothing. They laugh and talk about their wretchedness and poverty. If the priest reproaches them for some sin that he has seen them commit, they give alibis and plead their case, they blame their neighbors and accuse everyone but themselves. In short, they do everything in the confessional but what they are supposed to do, which is to state their sins with sincere contrition. They praise evil as well as good, minimize their faults, and whisper their most serious sins between clenched teeth for fear that the priest might hear what they are saying. Seeking to deceive him, they deceive themselves."

summarily beheaded. Abortion was not a political issue because any single woman discovered with child was drowned. (So, if he could be identified, was her impregnator.) . . . The ultimate crime, of course, was heresy. . . . Anyone whose church attendance became infrequent was destined for the stake [where they would be burned alive].[95]

Religious Persecution

Both Catholics and Protestants used such punishments to maintain control over the faithful. They also fought each other for control of entire cities or even countries. For example, Catholics and Protestants in the Netherlands fought a bloody civil war that lasted from 1568 to 1578.

In addition, the Catholic Church enacted certain reforms to try to retain control over people's beliefs and money. For example, the pope became more austere and ordered other clergymen to do the same. One sixteenth-century man wrote: "The pope is determined to live a monk's life. He has had all carpets and ornaments removed from his rooms. In his bedchamber nothing remains but a bedstead, a table, and several skulls."[96]

The church also began to persecute those who promoted Protestantism. In 1542 Pope Paul III established the Roman Inquisition, which had judicial authority over all Catholics living in Catholic countries. The Inquisition was charged with investigating and trying cases of heresy, and the guilty were subject to punishment ranging from penance to excommunication to execution.

According to Manchester, under the Inquisition, people faced horrible consequences for advancing Protestantism in any form. For example, in France,

The printing, sale, or even the possession of Protestant literature was a felony; advocacy of heretical ideas was a capital offense; and informers were encouraged by assigning them, after convictions, one-third of the condemneds' goods. Trials were conducted by a special commission, whose court came to be known as *le chambre ardente*, the burning room. In less than three years the commission sentenced sixty Frenchmen to the stake.[97]

But despite this religious persecution, Protestantism quickly replaced Catholicism in

Reforming the Church

In 1498 Girolamo Savonarola, an influential and zealous Italian Dominican priest, wrote to the sovereigns of France, Spain, Germany, and Hungary asking them to call a council on church reform. Historian Will Durant, in The Renaissance, *quotes Savonarola.*

"The moment of vengeance has arrived. . . . The Church is all teeming with abomination, from the crown of her head to the soles of her feet; yet not only do ye apply no remedy, but ye do homage to the cause of the woes by which she is polluted. Wherefore the Lord is greatly angered, and hath long left the Church without a shepherd. . . . For I hereby testify . . . that this Alexander is no pope, nor can be held as one; inasmuch as, leaving aside the mortal sin of simony, by which he hath purchased the papal chair, and daily selleth the benefices of the Church to the highest bidder, and likewise putting aside his other manifest vices, I declare that he is no Christian, and believes in no God."

Heretics are publicly condemned by an official of the Inquisition. The Catholic Church used the Inquisition to prevent the spread of the Protestant faith in Europe.

many parts of Europe. During the first half of the sixteenth century, England, Norway, Sweden, Denmark, and the Netherlands became Protestant countries. Most of Prussia, Germany, and Scotland also became Protestant, as did large areas of France and Switzerland.

The Church and the State

This rapid spread was partly due to the fact that many powerful people supported the dissolution of the Catholic Church, but on secular, or nonreligious, grounds. Manchester explains that after severing ties with the pope, monarchs typically began to "appropriate all Church wealth within their domains. . . . This was a powerful incentive to break with Rome; overnight a prince's tax revenues increased enormously."[98]

For example, in England between 1535 and 1539, King Henry VIII closed all monasteries and convents, selling or awarding their lands to members of the middle and upper classes. The king had several reasons for doing this, but historian G. R. Elton believes it occurred primarily because "the Crown needed money and the gentry needed lands."[99]

As part of this dissolution, Henry created the Church of England, with himself at its head instead of the pope. It combined aspects of both Catholicism and Protestantism; for

Religious Persecution

Those who practiced new religions were often called heretics and executed for their beliefs. Therefore many lived in hiding. One such person was Menno Simons, a sixteenth-century Anabaptist preacher. In his book The Renaissance and the Reformation, *Henry Lucas quotes Simons.*

"For eighteen years now I, my poor feeble wife and little children have endured extreme anxiety, oppression, affliction, misery, and persecution; and at the peril of my life have been compelled everywhere to live in fear and seclusion; yea, while the state ministers repose on beds of ease and of soft pillows we generally have to hide ourselves in secluded corners; while they appear at weddings and banquets with great pomp, with pipe and lute, we must be on guard when the dogs bark lest the captors be on hand. Whilst they are saluted as doctors, lords, and teachers on every hand, we have to hear that we are Anabaptists, hedge preachers, deceivers and heretics, and must be saluted in the name of the devil. In short, while they are gloriously rewarded for their services with large incomes and easy times, our recompense and portion must be fire, sword, and death."

example, worshipers continued to practice confession and communion, but religious services were simplified. However, as Protestantism gained hold in the country under the reign of Henry's daughter, Elizabeth I (1558–1603), many people argued that all Catholic elements should be eliminated from the Church of England in order to "purify" it. These dissidents were called Puritans.

Puritans were not allowed to form their own church because, by law, everyone in England had to attend the Church of England. In fact, throughout Europe, the spread of Protestantism did not mean that countries had more than one established church. For example, when Denmark and Norway adopted Lutheranism, the state church became Lutheran. Elton explains: "This was the age of uniformity, an age which held at all times and everywhere that one political unit could not comprehend within itself two forms of belief or worship."[100]

Moreover, Protestantism was not the only religion to spread during this period. Catholicism also gained many new adherents, primarily New World converts in lands claimed by Catholic explorers. As the merchant society looked for additional sources of wealth, it began to sponsor expeditions to distant lands, and the Catholic Church benefited from this expansion. By converting native peoples to Catholicism, the church was able to extend its reach even as its influence in Europe was declining.

New Sources of Wealth: Exploration and Conquest

The Renaissance is also called the Age of Exploration or the Age of Expansion because so many new worlds were discovered and colonized between 1450 and 1650. This phenomenal period of exploration and conquest was a natural consequence of the growing merchant economy. As trade and commerce became more lucrative, people wanted to find faster trade routes to known countries and to discover new lands in order to exploit their resources. As historian John Hale explains, exploration "was above all a thoroughly practical search for useful products, especially gold and spices."[101]

Portuguese Technology

Exploration was typically sponsored by wealthy merchants or monarchs who wanted to increase their fortunes. In fact, the first major supporter of exploration was a Portuguese prince who came to be known as Prince Henry the Navigator. The third son of King John I, Prince Henry participated in the Portuguese conquest of Ceuta, a coastal city in Morocco, in 1415. When Moroccan traders told him about a huge source of gold far south of their country, he decided to sponsor several sailing expeditions down the western African coast to find it.

But first he set up his own court, the Vila do Infante, on a rocky promontory called Sagres at the southwestern tip of Portugal. There he gathered experts in navigation, ship design, astronomy, and mapmaking, from whom came many new ideas. For example, they developed a technique that enabled sailors to find latitude when they could not see land, using the polestar, or North Star, as a guide. They also created tables that allowed sailors to determine latitude when the polestar was not visible, by making various calculations related to the sun's altitude.

In addition, Henry's experts advanced shipbuilding techniques. Portuguese fishermen had already invented a new kind of ship called the caravel; it had a rudder in its stern, giving it more stability in rough seas, and triangular sails, which allowed it to take advantage of crosswinds as well as headwinds and tailwinds. But under the guidance of Prince Henry, the caravel was further improved. Equipped with three masts, with a combination of square and triangular sails, and made lighter while remaining sturdy, the vessel was better suited for long-distance exploration than its predecessor, the galley.

The galley was designed with a side rudder that left the water when the hull rolled, so it was fairly unstable. It also had only one rectangular sail, because it was propelled primarily by oarsmen. In fact, some large war galleys required as many as two hundred oarsmen, and in times of plague it was difficult to find enough men to row it. A galley also had to carry a large number of armed soldiers to protect its cargo, while caravels had cannons mounted on the sides of their decks and therefore needed only a few men to defend against attack.

The triangular sails of the common caravel were augmented by square sails to help catch wind from many directions. This improved the ship's ability to make long-distance voyages.

For these reasons, caravels quickly replaced galleys in many parts of Europe. In addition, shipbuilders continued to improve on the caravel's basic design. Hale explains:

> Size and cargo capacity more than doubled; the canvas tarpaulin used to shelter the goods gave way to permanent wooden decks. . . . Bow and stern were built up into "castles" from which marines could shoot down onto an enemy deck during naval battles; they also protected against pirates and mutinies within the ship's own crew. The overall result: a sturdy little vessel that could go anywhere and defend itself in any company.[102]

Sailing to the East Indies

While Prince Henry's experts continued to improve navigational equipment and ship design, he began launching expeditions from Sagres. He chose from among the bravest men, because many people in this time of superstition and belief in magic had misconceptions about Africa. John Hale reports:

> It was widely believed that life was insupportable near the equator. Cape Nun, on the northwestern coast of Africa in latitude 29° north, was so named because of the legend that none of the seamen who ventured past it returned: beyond Cape Nun, it was rumored, the boiling sea destroyed all who were not already burned black by the vertical sun. Farther yet lay the Antipodes, where, according to many Churchmen, only monsters could live.[103]

However, as explorers sailed farther and farther south, these fears disappeared. Subsequent expeditions passed Cape Nun in 1434, and in 1473 crossed the equator. By this time, Prince Henry the Navigator had been dead for thirteen years, and a huge source of gold had still not been found. Nonetheless, African exploration proved lucrative, because the Portuguese had begun trading in African slaves.

They also continued to push their ships farther down the African coast. In 1488 Bartolomeu Dias rounded the southern tip of the continent and discovered its eastern shores. In 1497 Vasco da Gama went even farther, rounding Africa to cross the Indian Ocean and reach India.

Now Portugal could profit from the rich spice trade. Until this time, Muslim traders had completely controlled the transport of spices to Europe from the East Indies by way of the Middle East. But in 1512 Portugal captured the port of Melaka (or Malacca) in Malaysia, and soon dominated the region.

Meanwhile, King Ferdinand V and Queen Isabella I, the cosovereigns of Spain, decided to counter Portugal's activities and find their own sea route to the Indies. At first they tried to establish Spanish settlements along the African coast. However, the Portuguese claimed rights to the country, and the pope supported this claim. Then Ferdinand and Isabella decided to sponsor an Italian explorer, Christopher Columbus, who said he could find another way to the Indies. Columbus believed that the world was round, which meant that a sailor could reach the east by sailing west.

Columbus returned to the court of Ferdinand and Isabella with gifts and natives from the New World. The explorer's tales of vast gold deposits persuaded the king and queen to finance further expeditions.

On August 3, 1492, Columbus set sail across the Atlantic Ocean. His expedition comprised three ships: the *Niña* and *Pinta*, which were caravels, and the *Santa María*, which was a larger and less maneuverable version of the caravel called a carrack. All went fairly well until October 10, when the crew became afraid that they would never reach land. They asked Columbus to turn the ships around, but Columbus convinced them to wait three more days. Two days later, they spotted land: the island of San Salvador, in the Bahamas. Later they would reach the islands of Cuba and Hispaniola. In all of these places, Columbus noticed gold ornaments on the native people, many of whom he took back to Spain as slaves.

Shortly after his return in March 1493, Columbus told Ferdinand and Isabella that he had found incredible lands with vast resources of gold, and that he was sure he had reached China. They were persuaded to finance more expeditions across the Atlantic, as well as explorations of North and South American inte-

riors. The king and queen also convinced the pope to grant Spain possession of the entire region, just as he had done for Portugal when that country wanted Africa, so that no other Catholic country would usurp its claims.

Secrecy

As they amassed great wealth from exploration, Spain and Portugal tried to keep other countries from finding out about their voyages, for example, by making it illegal for a ship's pilot on a government expedition to share his rutters with anyone. Rutters were logbooks in which the pilot laboriously recorded the details of his vessel's travels, and as exploration increased they became extremely valuable documents. Manchester explains why:

> When . . . [an expedition] reached strange lands and returned—these records, or rutters, became invaluable. Each was a de-

Poor Treatment of Natives

Explorers who discovered new lands often took their natives as slaves. They did not treat these people well. In fact, in his book The Age of Exploration, *historian John Hale suggests that Renaissance men did not view non-Christians as human beings.*

"Europeans [treated natives with] deliberate savagery. A German, Ambrose Alfinger, exploring Venezuela in 1530, bound his Indian porters together with a chain bolted to iron rings clamped round their necks. If a slave was too exhausted to carry on, his head was cut off to avoid the delay of removing the collar. . . . In the lovely Marquesas Islands of the South Pacific, one . . . [European sailor] shot a native who, in fear, had jumped into the sea, a child in his arms. The sailor explained 'that he acted as he did lest he should lose his reputation as a good marksman.' . . . Episodes like [explorer Vasco] Da Gama's deliberate and pointless firing of a ship containing women and children are salutary reminders that cruel punishments and cruel sports were part of life in Renaissance Europe, and that to most explorers the killing of a non-Christian was more like stamping out vermin than it was like murder."

tailed, step-by-step chronicle of the journey out and the journey back. Specific information included tides, reefs, channels, magnetic compass bearings between ports and headlands, the strength and direction of winds, the number of days a master kept his vessel on each tack, when he heeled it over for repairs, where he found fresh water, soundings measured in fathoms and speed in knots, measured by comparing the time required for a sandglass to empty with the progress of knots which were tied, at intervals, on a rope attached to a small log that was thrown overboard and paid out. Everything went in, *everything*—even the changing color of the sea—which might conceivably be useful to another pilot trying to reach the same destination.[104]

But despite attempts at secrecy, word of Spain's and Portugal's discoveries soon spread to the rest of Europe:

Foreign merchants in [the Portuguese and Spanish trading cities of] Lisbon and Seville saw returning vessels unload the cargoes of spices, ivory, slaves and dyes; listened to seamen's gossip; bribed pilots and copied maps. All the information they gathered was sent home. Governments were fired by the thought of new riches and power, individuals saw a fresh path to wealth and adventure. First England, then France, then, toward the end of the 16th Century, the Netherlands entered the lists until exploration became a European movement.[105]

An explorer's crew was relatively easy to bribe because sailors did not earn a lot of money. Hale says: "The gold their captains sought would go to the Crown, and on a voy-

Experienced sea captains like the one pictured were needed by European monarchs to head voyages to the New World. It was the skilled navigator, however, who was the most prized individual aboard ship.

age of discovery there was little chance of loot or a division of prize money from a captured treasure galleon."[106]

A Sailor's Life

At the same time, a sailor's life entailed a great deal of risk and hardship. Most spent months or years at sea, often in unknown waters where storms and shipwrecks were common; in fact, the *Santa María* sank during Columbus's voyage. This is one reason why most ships sailed in groups of two to four.

In addition, ships were very unsanitary places to live. Marzieh Gail reports:

Ship's Stores

In his book The Age of Exploration, *John Hale reprints the following list of provisions taken on a seventeenth-century voyage of exploration; these supplies were intended to feed 190 men for three months, by which time the captain counted on finding land and replenishing his stores.*

"8,000 pounds of salt beef
2,800 pounds of salt pork
A few beef tongues
600 pounds of haberdine (salt cod)
15,000 brown biscuits
5,000 white biscuits
30 bushels of oatmeal

40 bushels of dried peas
1-1/2 bushels of mustard seed
1 barrel of salt
100 pounds of suet
1 barrel of flour
11 firkins (small wooden casks) of butter
1 hogshead (large cask) of vinegar
10,500 gallons of beer
3,500 gallons of water
2 hogsheads of cider

Captain's Stores:
Cheese, pepper, currants, cloves, sugar, aqua vitae, ginger, prunes, bacon, marmalade, almonds, cinnamon, wine, rice"

Not much was done to keep either the ship or the crew clean. There was nothing but cold salt water for either bathing or laundry, and no tubs, so that sailors turned the job over to nature for long periods, and waited for rain. Beards were allowed to grow; feet were bare and unwashed, and clothes were often in tatters since each man furnished his own.[107]

The master or captain of a ship had a private cabin, but common sailors had to sleep down in the hold. However, this area was often damp, smelly, and rat infested. Hale explains: "All the ships leaked; even with regular use of the pumps, water was constantly sloshing in the bilge which was further fouled by the casual sanitary habits of the age."[108] Not surprisingly, in good weather most sailors preferred to sleep on deck.

The supplies stored in the hold included plenty of wine, which was preferred to water, and hard biscuits, as well as dried or salted foods such as peas, beans, fish, pork, and beef. Some ships also carried live animals, such as pigs, chickens, or horses. However, on long voyages a ship's stores could easily run out or go bad. Antonio Pigafetta, a passenger on the ship of Portuguese explorer Ferdinand Magellan, wrote a famous account of a famine that occurred one year into his voyage:

[The crewmen] were three months and twenty days without eating anything (i.e., fresh food), and they ate biscuit, and when there was no more of that they ate the crumbs which were full of maggots and smelled strongly of mouse urine. They drank yellow water, already several days putrid. And they ate some of the hides that were on the largest shroud [a large rope] to keep it from breaking and that were very much toughened by the sun, rain and winds. And they softened them in the sea for four or five days, and then they put them in a pot over the fire and ate them and also much sawdust. A mouse would bring half a ducat or a ducat. The gums of some of the men swelled over their upper and lower teeth, so that they could not eat and so died. And nineteen men died from that sickness . . . and twenty-five or thirty were so sick that they could not help with arm or limb.[109]

Magellan's historic voyage lasted from August 10, 1519, to September 8, 1522. The expedition is significant not only for its length but because it was the first to circumnavigate the globe. Sponsored by Spain, it left from Seville with five ships and approximately 280 men, but due to a series of calamities that occurred after the sailors reached the Pacific Ocean, only one ship and 35 men returned. That one ship carried enough riches to pay for the entire expedition. However, Magellan did not live to see his expedition's success; in April 1521 he was killed in the Philippines by natives.

Portuguese explorer Ferdinand Magellan led the first expedition to circumnavigate the globe. Magellan, however, died before the voyage was completed.

Native Conquests

In most cases, however, it was the natives who suffered at the hands of the explorers. When a European power—particularly Spain—discovered a land rich in natural resources, it usually attacked and enslaved native populations. As historian Herbert J. Muller explains, "In Central and South America, where the Spaniards ran into civilizations rich in silver and gold, it was the metal that made the big difference"[110] in Spain's desire for conquest. The wealthy Aztec Empire of Mexico and Inca Empire of Peru were both destroyed by Spanish conquistadors during the early 1500s. Their lands were then mined for gold and silver using slave labor.

Native slaves were poorly treated. They were also exposed to European diseases against which they had no immunity. As a result, their populations declined drastically. For example, John McKay reports:

> Forced labor, disease, and starvation in the Spaniards' gold mines rapidly killed off the Indians of Hispaniola. When Columbus arrived in 1492, the population had been approximately 100,000; in 1570, 300 people survived. Indian slaves from the Bahamas and black Africans from Guinea were then imported to do the mining.[111]

Natives who survived Spanish or Portuguese conquest were immediately and aggressively converted to Catholicism. According to McKay, the prevailing view of Europeans was that "attitudes and values were shaped by religion and expressed in religious terms," and explorers from Spain and Portugal demonstrated a particularly "crusading fervor" in their desire to spread Old World religion among New World people.[112] To that end, "Once in America they urged home governments to send clerics."[113]

The French took a similar approach towards converting indigenous people, bringing Christian missionaries into the New World. However, their exploration was concentrated in upper North America and Canada. In the 1520s the French sponsored the voyages of Florentine explorer Giovanni da Verrazano, who discovered what is now the Carolina coast, New York harbor, and Maine. France also funded the voyages of Jacques Cartier, who sailed into Canada's St. Lawrence River in the 1530s.

The purpose of both of these expeditions was to try to find a northwest passage across the globe to the Indies. For the same reason, the English sponsored the voyages of the Italian Giovanni Caboto, known as John Cabot, who discovered Newfoundland in 1497. Unlike the Spanish and French, however, the English did not try to spread Christianity through their exploration. Herbert Muller says: "The self-righteous Protestant English made little effort to convert the Indians, sending out no such missionaries as the French to the north of them and the Spaniards to the south."[114]

However, Muller adds, the English had a valid reason for this: "They neglected to send out missionaries to the Indians . . . [because] they were busy making their own living, fashioning a new life for themselves."[115] He explains that whereas most Spanish settlers went to the New World specifically to seek fortunes and convert Indians, a large number of English settlers, such as the Puritans, went there to free themselves from religious persecution in Europe.

Challenges to Spain and Portugal

But the English also wanted to share in Spain's riches. For this reason, they sanctioned the privateering of Sir Francis Drake. Privateers captured enemy ships and cargoes in the name of their monarch, which meant that they turned

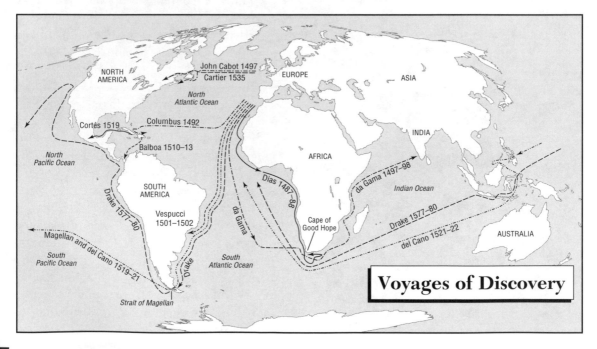

Voyages of Discovery

Scurvy

On long sea voyages, many sailors died of scurvy, a vitamin C deficiency prevented by eating fresh fruit, too often unavailable. In The Age of Exploration, *John Hale quotes one sixteenth-century sufferer's own description of the terrible disease.*

"It rotted all my gums, which gave out a black and putrid blood. My thighs and lower legs were black and gangrenous, and I was forced to use my knife each day to cut into the flesh in order to release this black and foul blood. I also used my knife on my gums, which were livid and growing over my teeth. . . . When I had cut away this dead flesh and caused much black blood to flow, I rinsed my mouth and teeth with urine, rubbing them very hard. . . . And the unfortunate thing was that I could not eat, desiring more to swallow than to chew. . . . Many of our people died of it every day, and we saw bodies thrown into the sea constantly, three or four at a time. For the most part they died with no aid given them, expiring behind some case or chest, their eyes and the soles of their feet gnawed away by the rats."

part of each stolen treasure over to their king or queen. In this way, a privateer was different from a pirate, who robbed every ship he encountered, regardless of its nationality, and kept all the treasure for himself.

Both piracy and privateering were common in the Renaissance, because so much valuable cargo was being transported by ship. Spanish vessels were particularly vulnerable; they were often attacked in the West Indies, the Caribbean, and along the coast of South America as they left shore loaded with gold, silver, and precious gems. But whereas piracy was always motivated by a desire for profit, privateering had a religious aspect. Historian Hamilton Cochran explains:

It is important to note that through the whole history of Western piracy and privateering runs the dark thread of religious antagonism. The religious conflict between the Protestants and Catholics of Europe in the 1500's and 1600's had an important bearing on the situation in the West Indies and Spanish America. The Spanish thought of themselves as defenders of the Roman Catholic religion and did everything they could to help other Roman Catholic governments against the growing forces of Protestantism which had

Sir Francis Drake was an English privateer who, during one of his voyages of sanctioned piracy, became the second explorer to circumnavigate the globe.

risen up in England, France, Germany, and Holland. . . . As a result of this, many privateering expeditions sent out by England (under such able commanders as Sir John Hawkins, Sir Francis Drake, and Sir Richard Grenville) were accused of Protestant piracy by the infuriated Spanish whose ships and towns they sacked.[116]

But whether the motive was religion or money, Cochran says that Sir Francis Drake held a "one-man war against Spain,"[117] making several expeditions to Spanish America as a privateer. His most important voyage began in December 1577 and lasted two years and ten months. During that time, Drake rounded Cape Horn, attacked Spanish cities on South America's western coast, pillaged their treasure, and sailed north to claim part of California for England. He then crossed the Pacific Ocean to reach England, becoming the first man since Magellan's voyage to circumnavigate the globe.

Although Drake had lost four ships along the way, his one remaining vessel, the *Golden Hind*, carried great wealth. Despite protests from Spain, an appreciative Queen Elizabeth knighted the privateer for his bravery in circling the globe. She then claimed a substantial part of his treasure for England.

As a result of such exploits, the relationship between England and Spain deteriorated, and eventually war broke out between the two countries. In July 1588 the fleet of the world's greatest naval power, the Spanish Armada, attacked the English coast. It left in defeat a month later. Only 76 of 130 Spanish ships returned home and England emerged a superior naval power whose dominance on the seas would continue for centuries.

Many more Spanish ships were destroyed before the war ended in 1604, crippling Spain's ability to defend its territories in the New World. The Dutch realized this, and seized the opportunity to begin challenging the dominance of both Spain and its ally Portugal in world trade.

In 1602 a group of Dutch merchants established the Dutch East India Company, a trading company with strong government support. It soon began taking over many Portuguese- and Spanish-held territories. For example, in 1619 it displaced the Portuguese from Java and much of Asia, and in 1641 it

Managing the New World

Christopher Columbus recorded his impressions of how the New World should be managed in this excerpt from a letter to Ferdinand and Isabella of Spain, reprinted in Kirkpatrick Sale's The Conquest of Paradise. *Dated November 27, 1492, the letter was written after his exploration of Cuba.*

"And Your Highnesses will command a city and fortress to be built in these parts, and these lands converted; and I assure Your Highnesses that it seems to me that there could never be under the sun [lands] superior in fertility, in mildness of cold and heat, in abundance of good and healthy water. . . . So may it please God that Your Highnesses will send here, or that there will come, learned men and they will see the truth of all. . . . And I say that Your Highnesses ought not to consent that any foreigner trade or set foot here except Catholic Christians, since this was the end and the beginning of enterprise . . . , that it was for the enhancement and glory of the Christian religion, nor should anyone who is not a good Christian come to these parts."

The powerful Spanish Armada set sail to attack England in 1588. Bad weather and superior English naval tactics, however, forced the crippled fleet to withdraw in defeat.

seized the rich spice port of Melaka. Meanwhile, Dutch explorers discovered Australia in 1606 and Tasmania and New Zealand in 1642. These new lands brought additional wealth into the Netherlands, and by the end of the Renaissance the Dutch had become Europe's largest importers and distributors of a variety of goods, including spices, sugar, porcelain, and decorative beads.

Expanding Knowledge

Exploration increased the economic strength of most merchant societies. It also brought exciting new information about strange lands and cultures. According to John McKay:

> Just as science fiction and speculation about life on other planets excite readers today, quasi-scientific literature

about Africa, Asia, and the Americas captured the imaginations of literate Europeans. Oviedo's *General History of the Indies* (1547), a detailed eyewitness account of plants, animals, and peoples, was widely read.[118]

Before explorers began venturing into uncharted waters, people's conceptions of the world were the products of centuries of myth and superstition. For example, they believed the world was flat and that the seas of the equator would boil a man alive. They believed that primitive lands would be filled with horrible monsters. But as sailors returned safely with information about their discoveries, bringing with them exotic goods and unknown plants, animals, and people, Renaissance society was forced to reassess its worldview. Perhaps the greatest riches of Renaissance exploration were not gold and silver but ideas.

The Renaissance Legacy: The Arts and Sciences

The Renaissance was an age of rapid dissemination of new information. This information was derived primarily from exploration and the scientific inquiry promoted by humanism. Explorers expanded knowledge by providing facts related to geography, botany, and zoology, and by encouraging the development of new technology related to trade and commerce. Humanists expanded knowledge by rediscovering ancient books that preserved lost ways of thinking about science, philosophy, and civilized society.

Scientific Advances

Many scientific advances came about because of the need for better navigational and sailing techniques. For example, Prince Henry the Navigator's scientists furthered the studies of astronomy and mathematics as they developed calculations for determining latitude and longitude, and in 1608 the Dutch invented the telescope, which enabled sailors to see great distances. Renaissance inventors also improved the windlass, a cranked winch used to hoist an anchor.

Other inventions came about because of trade and commerce. For example, shortly after gold and silver were discovered in the New World, the technology of the windlass was applied to the Spanish mining industry; windlasses with attached buckets were used to extract ore from the earth. The mining industry also inspired Renaissance inventors to create hoisting pumps to drain water from wells, boring machines, blast furnaces, and various new metallurgy techniques. In addition, in order to protect valuable cargo, they improved various types of artillery, and the use of gunpowder became widespread.

But inventions developed for sailors eventually benefited other aspects of society as well. For example, in 1609 Italian mathematics professor Galileo Galilei developed his

Italian scholar Galileo Galilei concluded that the sun was the center of the universe. Because the Catholic Church decreed that the sun revolved around the earth, Galileo was forced to publicly recant his findings.

Science Influenced by Religion

Scientists were often influenced by their religious beliefs, as this excerpt from Galileo Galilei's Treatise on the Universe *(1590), reprinted in Kenneth Atchity's* The Renaissance Reader, *illustrates.*

"I say . . . there must exist some first uncreated and eternal being, on whom all others depend, and to whom all others are directed as to an ultimate end. Proof of the first part of the conclusion: because otherwise it would follow that a thing would have produced itself, or that everything would have come into existence without an agent, and either is absurd. Proof of the second part: because there must be some first efficient cause of everything; but this cannot be other than a first and uncreated being; therefore all things will depend on, and be referred to, that being. . . . To anyone asking how much time has passed from the beginning of the universe, I reply: though Sixtus of Siena in his *Bibliotheca* enumerated various calculations of the years from the world's beginning, the figure we give is most probable and accepted by almost all educated men. The universe was created 5748 years ago, as is gathered from Holy Scripture."

own telescope, which was superior to the one invented in Holland. He presented it to the chief magistrate in Venice, Italy, for use in the city's merchant fleet. Later he made an even more powerful one for himself and used it to study the skies. He recorded his observations regarding planetary positions and cosmic phenomena like sunspots, the craters of the moon, the rings of Saturn, the satellites of Jupiter, and the stars of the Milky Way, publishing his findings in March 1610 as the *Sidereus nuncius*, or *Starry Messenger*.

Galileo also developed his own method of determining longitudes at sea, and he invented a new type of "compass" that was actually a crude calculator for computing mathematical problems. He worked with pendulums to study the laws of motion, and he explored the physics of tides and gravitational pull.

A Conflict in Beliefs

However, Galileo's research into tides and gravitation caused him a great deal of trouble.

It confirmed the findings of Polish astronomer Nicolaus Copernicus, published as *De revolutionibus orbium coelestrium*, or *On the Revolutions of the Heavenly Spheres*, which had been banned by the Catholic Church in 1616. Galileo was brought to trial as a heretic, and eventually the church forced him to recant his own defense of a Copernican solar system.

Copernicus's work was banned because it argued that the sun was stationary and the earth revolved around it. This concept, called Copernicanism, contradicted the church position that the earth was the center of the universe, and very few scholars accepted it. Far more believed in a model developed in 1588 by Danish astronomer Tycho Brahe. Brahe postulated that five planets revolved around the sun, and that this system revolved around the earth, which held a fixed position.

Belief in a fixed earth was important to Renaissance people, because they depended on astrology, which used the alignment of planets to predict future events. John Hale explains:

Astrologers taught in universities and received pensions from princely courts. . . . Governments took their advice (or at least asked for it) before sending an embassy, private individuals before laying the foundation stone of a house or before going on a journey. . . . The doctor picked his [medicines] and administered them at astrologically determined times. Farmers planted, reaped and slaughtered with . . . [astrological guidebooks] in mind. To shift the centre of the universe would be to upset the calculations of all those who foretold the future or chose auspicious times of the day or month.[119]

In an earth-centered universe, the positions of stars came to possess a prophetic significance. Astrologers who interpreted the meanings of these stellar alignments were respected and widely consulted members of society.

In addition, church persecution made it difficult if not dangerous to express new ideas. For this reason, Margaret Ashton calls the Renaissance "a pre-scientific age" when religious teachings "were more powerful than observation and experiment."[120] Similarly, Hale says that the word *scientia* "simply meant knowledge as a whole (or one of its parts), and those who studied . . . the nature of the physical world . . . put philosophy above investigation."[121] In other words, belief was more important than observation, which is why many Renaissance people were executed as witches or sorcerers without proof of their magic powers.

Medical Advances

A belief in magic also affected the medical profession. According to Hale, many doctors "sought explanations [for illnesses] in the stars rather than in the bloodstream, and preferred magical to clinical experiment."[122] Many illnesses were suspected of having a supernatural or spiritual rather than an organic cause. The sick often prayed to God for relief, relying on priests instead of doctors.

Because superstition was so widespread, new medical practices were slow to be accepted among the general population. Therefore, according to Ashton, "During the Renaissance, the gap between the theory of medicine and what doctors actually did was wider than at almost any other period of history."[123]

Nonetheless, improvements did occur. For example, Italian Girolamo Frascastoro discovered new treatments for infectious diseases such as syphilis. French physician Ambroise Paré developed a new surgical procedure whereby a patient's bleeding was stopped by tying off blood vessels rather than cauterizing them with boiling oil or hot metal.

Science and Witchcraft

Despite the scientific advances of the Renaissance, belief in witchcraft was widespread. The following passage, reprinted in Kenneth Atchity's The Renaissance Reader, *is an excerpt from a newsletter of the Fugger family in Schwab-Munchen, Germany, which describes the events related to a 1590 witch burning.*

"Last Wednesday the innkeeper's wife . . . and the baker's wife . . . were tried here for their misdeeds in witchcraft. Mine hostess [the innkeeper's wife] is a short, stout, seventy-year-old doxy, who had taken to her accursed witchery when eighteen years of age. This she has practiced fifty-two years, and it is easy to imagine what havoc she has wrought in such a long time. As the result of fervent petitioning, her sentence has been lightened inasmuch as she was first strangled and then only burned.

The other was only seduced to this work of the Devil by Ursula Kramer, who was the first to be executed here. So far, she has not perpetrated any sore misdeeds, but so much has she owned to, that her life is forfeit. Even on her day of judgment she still thought she could vindicate herself, and even at the place of execution I myself heard her say that she was dying innocent. Most unwillingly did she submit to her fate. But in the end she was reconciled to it and prayed long to God that He might pardon her misdeeds."

Belief in the power of witchcraft provoked local authorities to execute anyone accused of consorting with the devil. Many innocent women throughout western Europe were sentenced to death on the testimony of their neighbors.

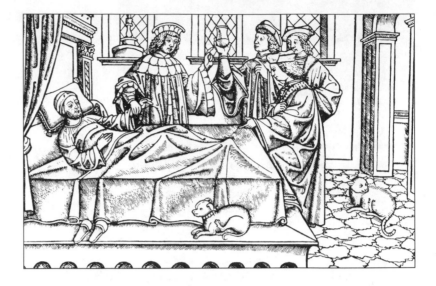

Although there were advances in medical scholarship during the Renaissance, a doctor's training and practice were still guided by superstitions and antiquated beliefs.

In 1543 Flemish scholar Andreas Vesalius wrote *De Humani Corporis Fabrica*, or *On the Fabric of the Human Body*, the first accurate anatomy text.

Vesalius's work was unique among European scholars, because he based it on his own detailed studies of human cadavers. At the time, most medical knowledge came from the recently translated works of two Greek physicians, Galen and Hippocrates.

Hippocrates, who lived from approximately 460 to 377 B.C., is considered the founder of medicine as a scientific discipline. He wrote about diseases, surgery, and bone fractures as well as anatomy, and taught his skills to others at the Hippocratic school in Cos, Greece. Galen, who lived from approximately A.D. 130 to 200, wrote more than five hundred treatises on physiology, hygiene, dietetics, pathology, pharmacology, and many other subjects, but his most important work was in anatomy. Dissecting both live and dead animals, he discovered that the spinal cord controls the movement of muscles, identified various nerves, demonstrated that the brain controls the voice, and proved that arteries carry blood rather than air. He also described the valves of the heart and determined the purpose of the kidney and bladder.

During the fifteenth and sixteenth centuries, the writings of Hippocrates and Galen were rediscovered, translated, and made widely available to Renaissance scholars. As a result, their findings were once again studied and discussed, which in turn led to new medical discoveries based on classical ideas. Similarly, the translation of classical Greek treatises on mathematics led to the solution of cubic equations. Ancient knowledge therefore advanced Renaissance science.

Advances in Art

Such knowledge also advanced Renaissance art. As society became interested in classical ideas, artists began to work in classical forms. For example, in the fifteenth century, the sculptor Donato di Niccolo di Betto Bardi, also known as Donatello, created the first life-size nude statue since ancient times. Named *David*, it was cast in bronze. Similarly, the Renaissance artist Pisanello revived the ancient Greek and Roman practice of putting faces on commemorative coins to honor important political figures, including members of the Medici family.

Renaissance artists also adopted classical subject matter as their own, depicting many figures from Greek and Roman mythology.

Not only did they show individual characters, but they created the narrative picture to display several characters interacting as part of a mythological scene. Their desire to accurately represent these scenes inspired them

Hospitals

By the standards of Renaissance health care, many hospitals were well run, particularly in Italy. In The Story of Civilization, *historian Will Durant quotes this description by Martin Luther, who visited several Italian hospitals in 1511.*

"In Italy the hospitals are handsomely built, and admirably provided with excellent food and drink, careful attendants, and learned physicians. The beds and bedding are clean, and the walls are covered with paintings. When a patient is brought in, his clothes are removed in the presence of a notary who makes a faithful inventory of them, and they are kept safely. A white smock is put on him, and he is laid on a comfortable bed, with clean linen. Presently two doctors come to him, and servants bring him food and drink in clean vessels."

Renaissance hospitals were generally clean and well managed, and they were a way to quarantine the sick.

to experiment with new artistic techniques. They developed new types of paint, discovered how to represent distance and three-dimensional space on a flat canvas, and learned to render landscapes more realistically. In addition, they used new knowledge about human anatomy to improve portrait painting.

But perhaps the most important advance for artists concerned attitude rather than tech-

Donatello's statue David *showed a revival of classical form. His sculpture was the first to copy the free-standing nudes of the Greeks and Romans.*

nique. During the Middle Ages, painting and sculpture were regarded as simple crafts, much like weaving or embroidery. However, in the Renaissance they were elevated to the level of art, much like writing or poetry. Artists consequently gained higher status in society.

Social Standing

In part, this change in status was the result of the new merchant economy. People with more money were more willing to spend it on art. For example, John Hale says that once the Dutch became wealthy traders,

> they spent the enormous profits from this trade on middle-class pleasures, filling their houses with valuable furnishings, wearing beautiful fabrics, loading tables with lavish meals. When such spending could not absorb all the money that poured in, they turned to art, which they often commissioned to commemorate themselves or their possessions. At first only by-products of prosperity, many of these paintings became the enduring monuments of . . . Dutch achievement.[124]

As the recipients of such largesse, artists experienced new levels of prosperity themselves. They also became highly respected members of their communities, and many middle- and upper-class fathers considered careers as painters and sculptors for their sons. When a boy reached the age of ten or eleven, his family would take samples of his artwork to a master's workshop to apply for an apprenticeship there.

The life of an apprentice was hard. In exchange for room, board, and lessons, he performed the many menial tasks of the workshop, essentially the master's servant. An

An artist paints while his apprentice performs tasks in the background. Apprentices performed menial services for their masters, hoping that in time they would be given greater responsibilities such as assisting in the actual painting of a work.

apprentice cleaned brushes, ground pigments to make paint, and mixed plaster. If he excelled at his art studies, eventually he was given more interesting tasks. Historian Marzieh Gail says: "The master would point out a corner of some large work and tell him to paint in a bit of background. Later, after years of training, when his brush had become swift and sure, the youth might be chosen as one of a team to paint a church fresco, a task where there was no place for mistakes and second tries."[125]

The period of apprenticeship typically lasted three years. After that, a young painter could remain at the master's shop as an employee or, if he obtained membership in a guild, he could open his own shop. However,

according to Peter Burke, "when an artist kept a shop . . . he had less economic security and a lower social status."[126] The best way for an artist to succeed was to attract a wealthy benefactor who would buy his work on a regular basis or even offer him complete economic support. Such a person was called a patron.

The Patronage System

During the Renaissance, the patronage system spread throughout Europe, offering artists increased security and prosperity. This in turn allowed them the freedom to experiment or pursue a personal vision.

There were primarily three sources of patronage: a wealthy individual, a guild, and the Catholic Church. Individual patrons were members of the middle class who wanted to gain prestige by offering economic support to artists. According to Burke, "rising families saw art patronage as a way of showing the world that they had reached the top."[127] Moreover, Gail says that "rich men today collect fine arts, but in the Renaissance they collected the artists themselves."[128]

This attitude led to many unique artist-patron relationships. For example, Gail reports:

> Andrea Mantegna, typical of many artists, stayed fifty years at the court of Mantua. He was paid fifteen ducats a month (about sixty dollars), besides getting wheat, wood, wine, and lodgings for himself and his family. Although often bad-tempered and given to complaining, he was tolerated as a valuable member of the household. Since artists might be loaned out by their patrons, the Pope borrowed Mantegna to paint a chapel, and the painter was away two years. Homesick, he wrote to say he was "a

Renaissance artists occasionally had eccentric work habits. Some practiced their art intermittently, being more interested in leisure than in painting or sculpture. Others were obsessed with their work, neglecting everything and everyone else. Peter Burke offers several examples of artistic quirks and quotes Italian Renaissance art historian Giorgio Vasari.

"Masaccio . . . was absent-minded (persona astratissima); 'Having fixed his mind and will wholly on matters of art, he cared little about himself and still less about others. . . . He would never under any circumstances give a thought to the cares and concerns of this world, nor even to his clothes, and was not in the habit of recovering his money from debtors.' . . . Paolo Uccello was so fascinated by his 'sweet' perspective that 'He remained secluded in his house, almost like a hermit, for weeks and months, without knowing much of what was going on in the world and without showing himself.' Vasari also gives a vivid account of the 'strangeness' of Piero di Cosimo, who was absent-minded, loved solitude, would not have his room swept, and could not bear children crying, men coughing, bells ringing or friars chanting."

child of the house of Mantua" and wished to come back.[129]

Similarly, the Italian master Leonardo da Vinci had the continuing patronage of Lodovico Sforza, the duke of Milan, who commissioned several works, including a portrait of the duke's mistress, an equestrian monument to the duke's father, and a collection of costumes and stages for court festivals; da Vinci also worked for the duke as a military engineer. The great Italian artist and sculptor Michelangelo was supported during part of his career by a member of the wealthy Medici family of Florence.

Commissioned Works

When merchant guilds acted as patrons, they typically commissioned public works such as a building or monument over which they had responsibility. For example, in Florence, the wool guild, charged with maintaining and beautifying the city's cathedral, commissioned statues for it from both Donatello and Michelangelo. Florence's cloth guild, which maintained the Baptistery, where babies were baptized, commissioned the sculptor Ghiberti to cast its massive bronze doors.

But the Catholic Church was the most important art patron. Historian Ernst Breisach reports: "The great artists and architects of the Renaissance, with few exceptions, worked for the popes on at least a few commissions."[130] One reason for this was the 1447 decision of Pope Nicholas V to rebuild Rome as a spectacular papal city. According to historian J. H. Plumb:

All the gold and silver of the West would scarcely have been sufficient for the multitude of churches, convents, monasteries, palaces, theaters, gardens, piazzas, towers, walls, and fortifications that [the pope's architects] planned. The cost did not daunt the Pope. He tore down the ancient Roman temples [of the old city] and began slowly to lay the foundations of [the new one].[131]

The papal city became a papal state, today the Vatican, and its construction involved many architects and artists working over decades. In addition to the buildings themselves, the church commissioned many new works of art to glorify its city. For example, Michelangelo's *Pietà* adorned the crowning glory of the papal state, the monumental rectangular basilica of St. Peter. He also spent four years painting biblical scenes on the ceiling of the Sistine Chapel, which was used for special ceremonies conducted by the pope.

Music

The patronage system brought Michelangelo and many other Renaissance painters and sculptors profitable work throughout their lifetimes. This was also true for some musicians. The Catholic Church commissioned singers to perform in its religious choirs. City governments or royal courts commissioned composers and instrumental musicians for state events, festivals, or private entertainment.

Flemish performers were particularly in demand throughout Europe, because they were reputed to be the best musicians. Consequently they attracted many important patrons. For example, both masters of the choir of the cathedral of St. Mark in Venice, Italy, were Flemish.

Music patronage evolved much as art patronage; as the middle classes grew wealthy, they spent more money on musical entertainment and on instruments they could play themselves at home. In fact, instruments became so popular in England that shops sometimes had them on hand for customers to play to pass the time while waiting. Throughout Europe, many new instruments began to appear for public enjoyment. For example, Renaissance Italians invented the violin, the spinet piano, and the harpsichord and also improved wind instruments.

Moreover, just as artists were inspired by a rediscovery of classical ideas, so too were musicians inspired by the ancient Greeks and Romans. John Hale reports that in 1581, Galileo's father wrote that the superior musical techniques of classical times, forgotten during the Middle Ages, had been rediscovered in the sixteenth century because man "began to investigate what music was and so seek to rescue it from the darkness in which it had been buried."[132]

Great literature was similarly inspired by classical models. Not only humanists but poets

Michelangelo was a master in many fields of study. He was commissioned as an architect, painter, and sculptor, but he also wrote poetry and theorized new mechanical inventions.

The Renaissance revived an interest in classical music and inspired the general public to purchase musical instruments for their personal use.

and playwrights drew on ancient Greek and Roman sources. English Renaissance playwright William Shakespeare based many works on themes and characters from ancient history and mythology.

Shakespeare wrote more than thirty-five histories, comedies, and tragedies, eighteen of which appeared in print during his lifetime. Along with his other writings, which consist of 154 sonnets and two narrative poems, these plays are considered among the greatest legacies of the Renaissance. They are still performed regularly today.

They were first presented in London's theaters, most famously the Globe theater, which opened in 1599. Prior to the sixteenth century, most plays were performed not in permanent theaters but on temporary stages in public squares, and no admission was charged. Instead these plays were funded by guilds, civic authorities, or religious leaders.

The Rise of Theaters

However, as the middle classes grew wealthier, performers saw an opportunity for greater profit through admission fees. Typically, a manager of a performing group would put up the capital to erect a permanent theater and then share the profits from ticket sales with his acting company. The first such building opened in London in 1576, in Madrid in the 1580s, and in Paris in 1599. Hale reports that in most places, including England, the public did not seem to mind the admission charges:

> At the large commercial theatres in London . . . , with their covered tiers of [seating] galleries rising around an open space for standing room, one penny was charged in the arena, from two to six, according to the proximity of the benches to the stage, for the galleries. In smaller, indoor, weatherproof theatres admission varied from six to thirty pence. When a penny was a day's wage for a skilled worker, the fact that London's theatres by 1605 could accommodate over eight thousand men and women at any one time points to drama's ability to retain an audience after the introduction of charges. Indeed, the anticipated audiences were larger than ever.[133]

Shakespeare was a member and part owner of the Globe's production company, and he utilized its unique design in his plays. Performances took place on a covered, three-level stage approximately forty feet wide. The lower level of the stage was divided into two parts: a twenty-seven-foot-deep outer area

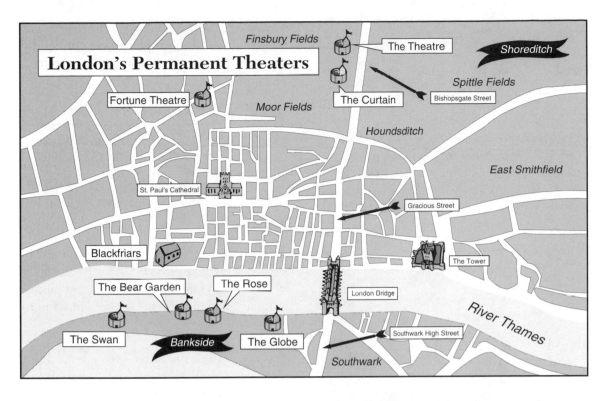

London's Permanent Theaters

Finsbury Fields

The Theatre

Shoreditch

Fortune Theatre

Moor Fields

The Curtain

Spittle Fields

Bishopsgate Street

Houndsditch

St. Paul's Cathedral

East Smithfield

Gracious Street

Blackfriars

The Tower

The Bear Garden

The Rose

London Bridge

The Swan

Bankside

The Globe

Southwark High Street

River Thames

Southwark

and a small, recessed inner area that could be concealed with curtains when not in use. The inner area also had two doors through which actors could walk. The second level of the stage had another small recessed area, this one with two windows and a balcony. The third level was the music gallery, but the front of this area could also be used as a staging area. Scenes were acted in each of these areas in succession; thus action was uninterrupted and no scenery changes were necessary.

The walls of the Globe formed the shape of a hexagon. Within this enclosed area was an uncovered courtyard, fifty-five feet wide, where people could stand to watch the performances; there were also seats along the perimeter in a covered gallery. In total, there was room for over fifteen hundred people in the Globe.

The theater was open every day except during the religious observations of Lent.

William Shakespeare was one of England's most prolific playwrights. He wrote more than thirty-five plays that greatly influenced the world's theatrical and literary traditions.

Some new medical practices were discovered by accident. For example, Ambroise Paré, a surgeon who lived from 1517 to 1590, made a startling discovery while treating patients during a French war. The tradition at the time was to pour boiling oil onto a wound to disinfect, or cauterize, it. But when he ran out of oil, he found out that something else worked better. Paré's description of what he discovered appears in Henry Lucas's book The Renaissance and the Reformation.

"At last my oil ran short, and I was forced instead thereof to apply a digestive [poultice] made of the yolk of eggs, oil of roses, and turpentine. In the night I could not sleep in quiet, fearing some default in not cauterizing, that I should find the wounded to whom I had not used the said oil dead from the poison of their wounds; which made me rise very early to visit them, where beyond my expectation I found that those to whom I had applied my digestive medicament had but little pain, and their wounds without inflammation or swelling, having rested fairly well that night; the others, to whom the boiling oil was used, I found feverish, with great pain and swelling about the edges of the wounds. Then I resolved never more to burn thus cruelly poor men with gunshot wounds."

Anyone of any social class could attend. In 1609 one London playwright observed: "your stinkard has the same liberty to be there in his tobacco-fumes which your sweet courtier hath, and . . . your car-man [cart-puller] and tinker . . . sits in judgement on the play's life and death."[134]

A Special Time

The theater was extremely popular among all levels of society because it was so accessible. Everyone, literate or not, could enjoy a good play. The same was true for music and art, when they were shared in public places.

As more people in European society were exposed to such cultural riches, and as they heard about scientific advances and saw many new inventions, they began to realize they were living in a wonderful era. In 1457 one Italian merchant wrote: "Our times since 1400 have greater reason to be contented than any other since Florence was founded."[135] In 1517 the scholar Erasmus remarked that "as if on a given signal, splendid talents are stirring."[136]

This perception among Renaissance people that they were living in a special time brought confidence and boldness to scholars, scientists, and artists alike, inspiring new levels of thought that far surpassed classical times. Therefore although ancient ideas were at first given more value than contemporary ones, by the end of the Renaissance much original work had been produced, thereby setting the stage for many advances of the seventeenth and eighteenth centuries.

The Originality of the Renaissance

Renaissance scholars acknowledged the debt they owed to classical literature and thought. They appreciated ancient Greek and Roman manuscripts, restoring them to prominence in their own society, and understood the importance of exposing themselves to different ways of thinking. As Renaissance scientist Vannoccio Biringuccio wrote: "I am certain that new information always gives birth in men's minds to new discoveries and so to further information."[137]

A Unique Age

However, Renaissance scholars also believed that their own time had much to offer human history. For example, in 1620, the scholar Alessandro Tassoni wrote in his *A Comparison Between Ancient and Modern Ingenuity:*

> What did the Greeks and Romans ever invent that can be compared with the printing press. . . . Let us pass on to the compass and to the nautical chart. . . . What glory is owed to him who taught the Portuguese to navigate to an unknown pole, from one horizon to another? . . . What invention so tremendous was ever imagined that could match that of our artilleries? . . . The telescope alone, with which you can see things fifteen or twenty miles away as though they were in front of you, and which discovers invisible stars in the sky, surpasses by far any Latin and Greek inventions that

Polish astronomer Nicolaus Copernicus discerned that the earth orbited the sun.

were discovered in the whole of their so-much celebrated course of years.[138]

Today the Renaissance is still hailed for its inventiveness. Many new tools and instruments appeared during the period, as well as technology related to shipbuilding, navigation, mining, and metallurgy. Scientific knowledge also advanced dramatically, not only because of ancient manuscripts but also because of original thought. There were many creative and bold men during the period, such as the astronomers Copernicus and Galileo, who presented new thoughts about the universe at a time when the Catholic Church was against them.

Skepticism and Confidence

The technology and ideas developed by such people also inspired increased exploration. According to John McKay, during the sixteenth and seventeenth centuries "European peoples had the intellectual curiosity, driving ambition, and scientific technology to attempt feats that were as difficult and expensive then as going to the moon is today."[139] Such exploits advanced Renaissance knowledge still further in the fields of geography, geology, botany, and zoology.

Moreover, like modern astronauts, sailors traveled to places reputed to be dangerous or nonexistent, and their safe return made many scholars question long-held beliefs about the nature of the world. Herbert Muller believes that this questioning, which he calls "the art of doubt," is one of the most significant developments of the Renaissance. He says that it led to "a basic skepticism in the scientific spirit" by leading scholars to demand objective evidence for belief, and that it is "implicitly hostile to an unreasoned faith, or to belief supported only by the authority of custom or tradition."[140] Therefore, in Muller's view, the art of doubt was a critical stepping-stone to the scientific revolution of the late seventeenth and eighteenth centuries.

Such skepticism also spread to other areas of the culture besides science. For example, more people began to question their religious beliefs and practices. They wondered whether priests were really necessary in order for them to talk to God. They scrutinized the Catholic clergy, realized that it was flawed, and tried to reform the church or establish new religions.

In fact, whereas medieval people generally accepted the status quo, Renaissance people were increasingly interested in improving their society. Reforms in the Catholic Church were just one example of this desire for betterment. Others include the tendency of peasants to revolt against injustices and of the middle class to take a more active role in government. In smaller ways, too, people challenged common practices and beliefs. Artists experimented with new mediums and forms of expression, producing work that was markedly different from that of medieval artists.

In part, this willingness to improve on things was born from humanism. As humanist teachers encouraged everyone to have faith in the powers of man as well as God, individuals became more self-confident and felt freer to experiment.

Economics and Education

Of course, these new levels of confidence did not reach every member of society. Many people in the lower classes were still economically, culturally, or physically oppressed, as were slaves and women. But among a cultured elite, which grew larger through a changing economic system, there were increased opportunities for personal expression.

However, there is no doubt that education was vital for success. As McKay explains: "The Renaissance continued the gulf between the learned minority and the uneducated multitude that has survived for many centuries."[141] For this reason, urban middle-class parents encouraged the spread of educational facilities, which improved overall reading and writing skills.

This urban middle class was another original aspect of the Renaissance. As society became less agrarian, more people moved to cities

Leaving Something for Posterity

Renaissance people wanted to leave something behind for posterity. In The Civilization of Europe in the Renaissance, *John Hale explains how this desire colored their perceptions of history and of time.*

"The notion of living within a separate historical period added a sharpness to men's awareness of time's passing. Thomas Kantzow wrote in the 1530s of [his historical writings] . . . that thanks to him, 'posterity will have a record of the country as it was in my time.' [Renaissance writer Girolamo] Cardano stressed that 'matters concerning contemporary society which are at present familiar to everyone should not just be mentioned in passing. This is how so many things of our historical past have been obscured.' His autobiography, from which this remark is taken, joined . . . a host of memoirs which . . . witnessed to an individual's wish to leave a stamp on times that were new and passing."

and started their own businesses. In the rich trading economy of the time, they were then able to gain wealth regardless of their social status. Consequently they became more materialistic and wanted to imitate the upper classes.

No longer were noblemen the only ones to wear expensive clothes, collect fine art, or live in beautiful houses. Wealthy merchants could also enjoy these things, and as they spent money on goods or services provided by poorer people, they distributed their wealth to lower levels of society, whose members in turn bought more luxury items. In this way, the rigid class distinctions of the Middle Ages gradually disappeared.

Human Thought

This expansion of wealth was yet another unique aspect of the Renaissance, but according to many historians it was not the period's most important legacy. The most common contemporary view is that the significance of the Renaissance is the way it continues to affect today's thinking. As Margaret Ashton states:

> Human nature may not change over the millennia, but ways of thinking and perceiving do. Our mental processes owe much to the Renaissance. It was a movement that was both born from and gave birth to an awareness of style—in literature, architecture, sculpture and painting—and through our understanding of the concept, it descended to us from that period.[142]

Ashton explains that the awareness of style leads us to be self-critical and to aspire to perfection, another distinctive Renaissance goal. Moreover, she says that in the Renaissance, "The pursuit of excellence through imitation, learning to follow ancient models of expression, promoted habits of comparison and self-awareness."[143]

Because they themselves were interested in the past, Renaissance people believed that whatever they created would be important to posterity. Painting portraits, recording histories, and making changes in society were all different reflections of this need to send part of the present into the future. Therefore, unlike the Middle Ages, the Renaissance saw no great loss of ancient knowledge or great literature. Similarly, today's society continues to preserve information for future generations.

Notes

Introduction: A Break with the Past: New Ideas and Beliefs

1. Kenneth J. Atchity, ed., *The Renaissance Reader.* New York: HarperCollins, 1996, pp. xiv–xv.
2. John P. McKay, Bennett D. Hill, and John Buckler, *A History of Western Society*, vol. 1, *From Antiquity to the Enlightenment*. Boston: Houghton Mifflin, 1991, p. 394.

Chapter 1: Manorial Duties: The Relationship Between Rural Peasants and Nobles

3. William Manchester, *A World Lit Only by Fire: The Medieval Mind and the Renaissance.* Boston: Little, Brown, 1993, p. 50.
4. McKay, Hill, and Buckler, *A History of Western Society*, p. 249.
5. Irma Simonton Black, *Castle, Abbey, and Town.* New York: Holiday House, 1963, pp. 76–77.
6. McKay, Hill, and Buckler, *A History of Western Society*, p. 291.
7. Henry Lucas, *The Renaissance and the Reformation.* New York: Harper & Row, 1960, p. 481.
8. J. R. Hale, *Renaissance Europe.* Berkeley and Los Angeles: University of California Press, 1977, p. 202.
9. Quoted in Philippe Aries and Georges Duby, eds., *A History of Private Life*, vol. 3, *Passions of the Renaissance.* Cambridge, MA: The Belknap Press of Harvard University Press, 1989, p. 47.
10. McKay, Hill, and Buckler, *A History of Western Society*, p. 360.
11. McKay, Hill, and Buckler, *A History of Western Society*, p. 361.
12. Quoted in Aries and Duby, *A History of Private Life*, p. 339.
13. Manchester, *A World Lit Only by Fire*, p. 54.
14. McKay, Hill, and Buckler, *A History of Western Society*, p. 287.
15. McKay, Hill, and Buckler, *A History of Western Society*, p. 287.
16. Philippe Erlanger, *The Age of Courts and Kings: Manners and Morals 1558–1715.* New York: Harper & Row, 1967, p. 114.
17. Erlanger, *The Age of Courts and Kings*, p. 153.
18. Manchester, *A World Lit Only by Fire*, p. 53.
19. Manchester, *A World Lit Only by Fire*, pp. 53–54.
20. Quoted in Manchester, *A World Lit Only by Fire*, p. 53.
21. McKay, Hill, and Buckler, *A History of Western Society*, p. 286.
22. Quoted in Sarah Howarth, *Renaissance Places*. Brookfield, CT: Millbrook Press, 1992, p. 43.
23. Howarth, *Renaissance Places*, p. 43.
24. McKay, Hill, and Buckler, *A History of Western Society*, p. 389.

Chapter 2: Distributing Wealth: The Rising Middle Class

25. Manchester, *A World Lit Only by Fire*, p. 235.
26. Quoted in Erlanger, *The Age of Courts and Kings*, p. 233.
27. McKay, Hill, and Buckler, *A History of Western Society*, p. 404.

28. John Hale, *The Civilization of Europe in the Renaissance*, New York: Atheneum, 1994, pp. 44–45.
29. Erlanger, *The Age of Courts and Kings*, p. 48.
30. Erlanger, *The Age of Courts and Kings*, p. 23.
31. Erlanger, *The Age of Courts and Kings*, p. 22.
32. Manchester, *A World Lit Only by Fire*, p. 55.
33. Margaret Ashton, ed., *The Panorama of the Renaissance*. New York: Harry N. Abrams, 1996, pp. 93–94.
34. Manchester, *A World Lit Only by Fire*, p. 50.
35. Ashton, *The Panorama of the Renaissance*, p. 189.
36. Quoted in Erlanger, *The Age of Courts and Kings*, p. 94.
37. McKay, Hill, and Buckler, *A History of Western Society*, p. 333.
38. Erlanger, *The Age of Courts and Kings*, p. 41.
39. McKay, Hill, and Buckler, *A History of Western Society*, p. 333.
40. Marzieh Gail, *Life in the Renaissance*. New York: Random House, 1968, pp. 55–56.
41. Erlanger, *The Age of Courts and Kings*, p. 48.
42. Erlanger, *The Age of Courts and Kings*, p. 48.
43. Erlanger, *The Age of Courts and Kings*, p. 57.
44. Margaret L. King, *Women of the Renaissance*. Chicago: University of Chicago Press, 1991, pp. 27–28.
45. King, *Women of the Renaissance*, p. 28.
46. McKay, Hill, and Buckler, *A History of Western Society*, p. 336.
47. Lucas, *The Renaissance and the Reformation*, p. 338.

48. Lucas, *The Renaissance and the Reformation*, p. 163.
49. McKay, Hill, and Buckler, *A History of Western Society*, p. 389.
50. Christopher Hibbert, *The House of the Medici: Its Rise and Fall*. New York: William Morrow, 1975, p. 28.
51. Manchester, *A World Lit Only by Fire*, p. 98.
52. Hibbert, *The House of the Medici*, p. 25.
53. Hale, *Renaissance Europe*, p. 150.
54. Gail, *Life in the Renaissance*, p. 79.

Chapter 3: The Power of Knowledge: Education and Humanism

55. Hale, *Renaissance Europe*, pp. 152–53.
56. Lucas, *The Renaissance and the Reformation*, p. 182.
57. Lucas, *The Renaissance and the Reformation*, p. 181.
58. Hale, *Renaissance Europe*, pp. 283–84.
59. Quoted in Aries and Duby, *A History of Private Life*, pp. 115–16.
60. Hale, *Renaissance Europe*, p. 283.
61. Manchester, *A World Lit Only by Fire*, p. 97.
62. Quoted in King, *Women of the Renaissance*, p. 175.
63. King, *Women of the Renaissance*, p. 171.
64. Hale, *The Civilization of Europe in the Renaissance*, p. 194.
65. Hale, *The Civilization of Europe in the Renaissance*, p. 194.
66. Hale, *Renaissance Europe*, p. 284.
67. Howarth, *Renaissance Places*, p. 26.
68. Louis B. Wright, *The Renaissance: Maker of Modern Man*. Washington, DC: National Geographic Society, 1970, p. 17.
69. Quoted in Lucas, *The Renaissance and the Reformation*, p. 230.
70. Howarth, *Renaissance Places*, p. 26.
71. Hale, *Renaissance Europe*, p. 189.

72. Hale, *The Civilization of Europe in the Renaissance*, p. 195.
73. McKay, Hill, and Buckler, *A History of Western Society*, p. 394.
74. Wright, *The Renaissance*, pp. 17–18.
75. McKay, Hill, and Buckler, *A History of Western Society*, p. 405.
76. Ernst Breisach, *Renaissance Europe: 1300–1514*. New York: Macmillan, 1973, p. 279.
77. Hale, *Renaissance Europe*, p. 285.
78. Hale, *Renaissance Europe*, p. 286.
79. Hale, *Renaissance Europe*, p. 286.
80. Hale, *Renaissance Europe*, p. 287.
81. Howarth, *Renaissance Places*, p. 27.

Chapter 4: Struggling to Maintain Control: The Church in Daily Life

82. Quoted in George Holmes, *The Oxford Illustrated History of Medieval Europe*. London: Oxford University Press, 1988, p. 331.
83. Quoted in Aries and Duby, *A History of Private Life*, p. 74.
84. Manchester, *A World Lit Only by Fire*, p. 40.
85. Manchester, *A World Lit Only by Fire*, p. 41.
86. Quoted in Erlanger, *The Age of Courts and Kings*, p. 96.
87. Breisach, *Renaissance Europe*, p. 126.
88. Quoted in Aries and Duby, *A History of Private Life*, p. 100.
89. Quoted in Aries and Duby, *A History of Private Life*, p. 71.
90. Quoted in Aries and Duby, *A History of Private Life*, p. 72.
91. Quoted in Aries and Duby, *A History of Private Life*, p. 80.
92. Quoted in Aries and Duby, *A History of Private Life*, p. 85.
93. Manchester, *A World Lit Only by Fire*, p. 190.
94. Manchester, *A World Lit Only by Fire*, p. 191.
95. Manchester, *A World Lit Only by Fire*, pp. 191–93.
96. Quoted in Howarth, *Renaissance Places*, p. 39.
97. Manchester, *A World Lit Only by Fire*, pp. 201–202.
98. Manchester, *A World Lit Only by Fire*, p. 175.
99. G. R. Elton, ed., *The New Cambridge Modern History*, vol. 2, *The Reformation*. Cambridge: Cambridge University Press, 1990, p. 272.
100. Elton, *The New Cambridge Modern History*, p. 5.

Chapter 5: New Sources of Wealth: Exploration and Conquest

101. Hale, *Renaissance Europe*, p. 47.
102. John R. Hale and Time-Life Books, *The Age of Exploration*. New York: Time-Life Books, 1967, p. 85.
103. Hale, *The Age of Exploration*, p. 33.
104. Manchester, *A World Lit Only by Fire*, pp. 237–38.
105. Hale, *The Age of Exploration*, p. 19.
106. Hale, *The Age of Exploration*, p. 15.
107. Gail, *Life in the Renaissance*, pp. 154–55.
108. Hale, *The Age of Exploration*, p. 80.
109. Paula Spurlin Paige, trans., *The Voyage of Magellan: The Journal of Antonio Pigafetta*. Englewood Cliffs, NJ: Prentice-Hall, 1969, pp. 24–25.
110. Herbert J. Muller, *Freedom in the Western World: From the Dark Ages to the Rise of Democracy*. New York: Harper & Row, 1963, p. 362.
111. McKay, Hill, and Buckler, *A History of Western Society*, p. 461.
112. McKay, Hill, and Buckler, *A History of Western Society*, p. 463.

113. McKay, Hill, and Buckler, *A History of Western Society*, p. 465.
114. Muller, *Freedom in the Western World*, p. 363.
115. Muller, *Freedom in the Western World*, p. 364.
116. Hamilton Cochran, *Pirates of the Spanish Main*. New York: Golden Press, 1961, pp. 15–16.
117. Cochran, *Pirates of the Spanish Main*, p. 26.
118. McKay, Hill, and Buckler, *A History of Western Society*, pp. 464–65.

Chapter 6: The Renaissance Legacy: The Arts and Sciences

119. Hale, *Renaissance Europe*, pp. 314–15.
120. Ashton, *The Panorama of the Renaissance*, p. 216.
121. Hale, *Renaissance Europe*, p. 310.
122. Hale, *Renaissance Europe*, p. 138.
123. Ashton, *The Panorama of the Renaissance*, p. 224.
124. Hale, *The Age of Exploration*, p. 39.
125. Gail, *Life in the Renaissance*, pp. 118–19.
126. Peter Burke, *The Italian Renaissance: Culture and Society in Italy*. Princeton, NJ: Princeton University Press, 1986, p. 96.
127. Burke, *The Italian Renaissance*, p. 97.
128. Gail, *Life in the Renaissance*, pp. 119–20.
129. Gail, *Life in the Renaissance*, p. 121.
130. Breisach, *Renaissance Europe*, p. 125.
131. J. H. Plumb, *The Italian Renaissance*. Boston: Houghton Mifflin, 1987, pp. 92–93.
132. Hale, *The Civilization of Europe in the Renaissance*, p. 587.
133. Hale, *The Civilization of Europe in the Renaissance*, p. 278.
134. Quoted in Hale, *The Civilization of Europe in the Renaissance*, p. 278.
135. Quoted in Hale, *The Civilization of Europe in the Renaissance*, p. 585.
136. Quoted in Hale, *The Civilization of Europe in the Renaissance*, p. 585.

Epilogue: The Originality of the Renaissance

137. Quoted in Hale, *The Civilization of Europe in the Renaissance*, p. 590.
138. Quoted in Hale, *The Civilization of Europe in the Renaissance*, p. 589.
139. McKay, Hill, and Buckler, *A History of Western Society*, p. 494.
140. Muller, *Freedom in the Western World*, p. 257.
141. McKay, Hill, and Buckler, *A History of Western Society*, p. 399.
142. Ashton, *Panorama of the Renaissance*, p. 26.
143. Ashton, *Panorama of the Renaissance*, p. 28.

For Further Reading

Irma Simonton Black, *Castle, Abbey, and Town*. New York: Holiday House, 1963. This book for young readers deals primarily with the Middle Ages, but offers some insights into the development of Renaissance society.

Hamilton Cochran, *Pirates of the Spanish Main*. New York: Golden Press, 1961. For young readers, this well-illustrated book offers interesting information about Renaissance pirates and privateers in regions controlled by Spain.

Madeleine Pelner Cosman, *Medieval Wordbook*. New York: Facts On File, 1996. Interesting dictionary of words from the Middle Ages; many were also in use during the Renaissance.

Will Durant, *The Story of Civilization*. Vol. 5, *The Renaissance*. New York: Simon and Schuster, 1953. A lengthy discussion of art, music, and religion in Italy from 1304 to 1576, for more advanced readers.

Kathy Lynn Emerson, *The Writer's Guide to Everyday Life in Renaissance England from 1485–1649*. Cincinnati, OH: Writers Digest Books, 1996. Offers basic information about many aspects of Renaissance life in England, including clothing, money, and food.

Gertrude Hartman, *Medieval Days and Ways*. New York: Macmillan, 1937. Provides younger readers with a detailed discussion of life in the Middle Ages and early Renaissance.

Sarah Howarth, *Renaissance Places*. Brookfield, CT: Millbrook Press, 1992. This book for young people offers basic information about Renaissance society.

Peter James and Nick Thorpe, *Ancient Inventions*. New York: Ballantine Books, 1994. Traces the history of many inventions and activities throughout history, including weaponry, medical devices, zoos, theaters, and games.

Sherrilyn Kenyon, *The Writer's Guide to Everyday Life in the Middle Ages: The British Isles from 500 to 1500*. Cincinnati, OH: Writers Digest Books, 1995. Offers basic information about life in the Middle Ages, including housing, entertainment, and weaponry.

J. H. Plumb, *The Horizon Book of the Renaissance*. New York: American Heritage, 1961. Presents many excellent photographs of Renaissance art, as well as drawings of important individuals.

Jonathan Riley-Smith, ed., *The Oxford History of the Crusades*. Oxford: Oxford University Press, 1995. Many fine illustrations accompany a discussion of medieval and Renaissance religious wars.

A. L. Rowse, *The Elizabethan Renaissance: The Life of the Society*. New York: Charles Scribner's Sons, 1971. A detailed and interesting discussion of life in Renaissance England.

Carlos Alvarez Santalo, *The 15th Century*. Trans. Dorothy Hill. Madrid: Grupo Anaya, 1992. Uses a storytelling style to depict life in Europe during the 1400s.

Works Consulted

Philippe Aries and Georges Duby, eds., *A History of Private Life*. Vol. 3, *Passions of the Renaissance*. Cambridge, MA: The Belknap Press of Harvard University Press, 1989. A large collection of articles about family life, religious beliefs, and other personal aspects of the period.

Margaret Ashton, ed., *The Panorama of the Renaissance*, New York: Harry N. Abrams, 1996. More illustrations than text, this book has many fine photographs of Renaissance art and includes biographical sketches of many important Renaissance men and women.

Kenneth J. Atchity, ed., *The Renaissance Reader*. New York: HarperCollins, 1996. An anthology of various primary source documents and commentary.

Herschel Baker, *The Later Renaissance in England: Nondramatic Verse and Prose, 1600–1660*. Boston: Houghton Mifflin, 1975. A collection of writings from Renaissance England, including excerpts from the works of poet John Milton and essayist Sir Francis Bacon.

Morris Bishop, *The Middle Ages*. Boston: Houghton Mifflin, 1987. This volume in the American Heritage Library includes information about the dawn of the Renaissance.

Ernst Breisach, *Renaissance Europe: 1300–1514*, New York: Macmillan 1973. An in-depth discussion of the history and attitudes of the age.

Peter Burke, *The Italian Renaissance: Culture and Society in Italy*. Princeton, NJ: Princeton University Press, 1986. Although difficult reading, this study provides interesting information about Italian art, music, and culture.

Norman F. Cantor, ed., *The Medieval Reader*. New York: HarperCollins, 1994. A collection of writings from the Middle Ages and early Renaissance period.

G. R. Elton, ed., *The New Cambridge Modern History*. Vol. 2, *The Reformation*. Cambridge: Cambridge University Press, 1990. A detailed, scholarly text on the later Renaissance for advanced readers.

Philippe Erlanger, *The Age of Courts and Kings: Manners and Morals 1558–1715*, New York: Harper & Row, 1967. This interesting and informative book includes many quotations from Renaissance Europeans.

Marzieh Gail, *Life in the Renaissance*. New York: Random House, 1968. Describes daily life at all economic levels, offering details about such basic needs as housing, food, and clothing.

Frances and Joseph Gies, *Life in a Medieval Village*. New York: HarperCollins, 1990. Includes information pertinent to the early Renaissance regarding housing and rural life.

——, *Women in the Middle Ages*. New York: Barnes and Noble, 1978. Presents a solid background for the work of Margaret King, as presented in *Women of the Renaissance*.

John Hale, *The Civilization of Europe in the Renaissance*. New York: Atheneum, 1994. Includes some material from the author's previous work, *Renaissance Europe*, but offers additional quotations and information about Renaissance society.

J. R. Hale, *Renaissance Europe*. Berkeley and Los Angeles: University of California Press, 1977. Extremely informative and interesting, with sections on specific topics such as class structure, clerics, and universities.

John R. Hale and Time-Life Books, *The Age of Exploration*. New York: Time-Life Books, 1967. Offers many excellent illustrations and quotations regarding Renaissance exploration.

Christopher Hibbert, *The House of the Medici: Its Rise and Fall*. New York: William Morrow, 1975. This detailed text traces the rise of one of the most powerful families of the Italian Renaissance.

George Holmes, *The Oxford Illustrated History of Medieval Europe*. London: Oxford University Press, 1988. Contains many excellent illustrations of art and architecture from both the Middle Ages and the Renaissance.

Margaret L. King, *Women of the Renaissance*, Chicago: University of Chicago Press, 1991. A detailed discussion of women's lives in Europe between 1350 and 1650.

Henry Lucas, *The Renaissance and the Reformation*, New York: Harper & Row, 1960. Discusses Renaissance and Restoration history, politics, and culture, including details about many famous people of the period.

William Manchester, *A World Lit Only by Fire: The Medieval Mind and the Renaissance*. Boston: Little, Brown, 1993. An overview of the Renaissance, with an emphasis on human thought as it related to exploration and discovery.

John P. McKay, Bennett D. Hill, and John Buckler, *A History of Western Society*. Vol. 1, *From Antiquity to the Enlightenment*. Boston: Houghton Mifflin, 1991. A concise historical and cultural study of Europe to the eighteenth century.

Herbert J. Muller, *Freedom in the Western World: From the Dark Ages to the Rise of Democracy*. New York: Harper & Row, 1963. For more advanced readers, this text traces changes in human thought through the centuries.

Paula Spurlin Paige, trans., *The Voyage of Magellan: The Journal of Antonio Pigafetta*. Englewood Cliffs, NJ: Prentice-Hall, 1969. The journal of a Renaissance scholar who accompanied the explorer Magellan on his historic voyage around the world.

J. H. Plumb, *The Italian Renaissance*. Boston: Houghton Mifflin, 1987. This straightforward volume from the American Heritage Library describes various Italian cities and presents biographical chapters on some of the most famous Italians of the Renaissance.

Kirkpatrick Sale, *The Conquest of Paradise: Christopher Columbus and the Columbian Legacy*. New York: Plume (Penguin), 1991. An in-depth discussion of the explorer and the times in which he lived.

Kate Simon, *A Renaissance Tapestry: The Gonzaga of Mantua*. New York: Harper & Row, 1988. Detailed history of one important Renaissance family, the Gonzagas of Mantua, Italy.

Louis B. Wright, *The Renaissance: Maker of Modern Man*, Washington, DC: National Geographic Society, 1970. Includes many fine photographs and illustrations of Renaissance art and architecture.

Index

Picture Credits

About the Author

Patricia D. Netzley received a bachelor's degree in English from the University of California at Los Angeles (UCLA). After graduation she worked as an editor at the UCLA Medical Center, where she produced hundreds of medical articles, speeches, and pamphlets.

Netzley became a freelance writer in 1986. She is the author of several books for children and adults, including *The Assassination of President John F. Kennedy* (Macmillan/New Discovery Books, 1994), *Queen Victoria* (The Importance Of series, Lucent Books, 1996), *Alien Abductions* (Greenhaven Press, 1996), *Butch Cassidy* (Mysterious Deaths series, Lucent Books, 1997), *The Stone Age* (World History series, Lucent Books, 1998), and *The Environment* (Contemporary Issues series, Lucent Books, 1998). Her hobbies are weaving, knitting, and needlework. She and her husband, Raymond, live in southern California with their children, Matthew, Sarah, and Jacob.